Choosing Justice

California Series on Social Choice and Political Economy
Edited by Brian Barry, Robert H. Bates, and Samuel L. Popkin

Choosing Justice

An Experimental Approach to Ethical Theory

Norman Frohlich and Joe A. Oppenheimer

UNIVERSITY OF CALIFORNIA PRESS
BERKELEY LOS ANGELES LONDON

University of California Press
Berkeley and Los Angeles, California

University of California Press, Ltd.
London, England

© 1992 by
The Regents of the University of California

First Paperback Printing 1993

Library of Congress Cataloging-in-Publication Data
Frohlich, Norman.
    Choosing justice: an experimental approach to ethical theory/
Norman Frohlich and Joe A. Oppenheimer.
        p.   cm.—(California series on social choice and political
economy)
    Includes bibliographical references (p.) and index.
    ISBN 0-520-08437-3
1. Distributive justice. 2. Income distribution. 3. Social
choice.   I. Oppenheimer, Joe A.   II. Title.   III. Series.
HB523.F76 1992
330—dc20   91-29059
                                                                CIP

Printed in the United States of America
9 8 7 6 5 4 3 2 1

*For my parents, Israel and
Sarah Frohlich, who first
taught me about justice by
practicing it   N. F.*

*For all those whom I am
proud to call my teachers and
who taught me to struggle to
discover justice, especially my
mother, Dorothea K.
Oppenheimer   J. A. O.*

Contents

Figures and Tables

FIGURES

TABLES

Acknowledgments

We have many to thank. Cheryl Eavey was our coauthor in the early stages of this project. Before she pursued other interests, she presented us with valuable criticisms and suggestions regarding experimental design, ran some initial experiments, and participated in writing papers on our early results. Wlodzimirz Okrasa, Tadeus Tyszka, and Grzegorz Lissowski replicated our initial experiments in Poland. We greatly appreciate their permission to use their data in this comparative work.

Tom Schwartz first drew our attention to impartial reasoning as the core focus of our research. He also helped us in many other ways. Sam Popkin's encouragements to write the book and his constructive readings of early drafts were essential. Bill Galston gave us moral support and highly productive critiques regarding the conclusions. Michael Cain was most helpful in providing comments, especially regarding Chapter 1. Norman Schofield forced us to consider the role of robustness as an evaluative criterion of scientific theorizing. Gary Miller and Mark Winer helped us refine our debriefing instrument. Generous support by the Social Sciences and Humanities Research Council of Canada, by the National Science Foundation of the United States, and by our two universities made this work possible. Nuffield College of Oxford University provided a supportive atmosphere for work on the middle stages of the project, and the Associates of the Faculty of Management of the University of Manitoba supported travel for consultations in the final stages. We owe thanks to them too. A number of other readers of this manuscript gave us substantial help with their comments. We thank, especially, Dennis Mueller, Rick Uslaner, Karol Soltan, and Ron Terchek.

Research assistants, like diamonds, come in different grades. We were blessed with the best. They helped run experiments, comment on prototypes, scout out relevant materials, and check our analyses. For this help we thank Irvin Boschman, Michael Cain, Kevin Gunn, David Cross, Pam Edwards, Dennis Klimchuk, Valerie Lehr, Karen Loewen, Marilyn Erhardt, Judy Chipperfield, Paul Parker, Craig Conners, and Pat Bond.

Louise Hebert helped in typing and preparing the initial research instruments and has served as a key link in the communication chain between us.

SYSTAT, authored by Leland Wilkinson, gave us an ideal computing tool for our analysis.

Finally, very special thanks are owed to our wives, Roberta Frohlich and Bonnie Oppenheimer. They have been unwavering in their support of this project and have offered many helpful suggestions at all its phases.

Some of the research in this book has been reported elsewhere (see Frohlich, Oppenheimer, and Eavey 1987a and 1987b, and Frohlich and Oppenheimer 1989 and 1990). The results from Poland are reported in Lissowski, Tyszka, and Okrasa (1991).

Introduction:
Understanding
Distributive Justice

What is fair? What is just? And if there *are* answers to these questions, how can we come to know them? These are central concerns of ethical and political philosophers. For well over two thousand years, philosophers have been attempting (without notable success) to develop definitive answers to these questions. Their efforts bespeak the continuing appeal of the questions, but their failure to gain closure gives us pause. If great minds focusing on the problem for so long have not been able to find a solution, it may be useful to ask why.

We contend that ethicists have been unsuccessful because they have been using an inappropriate methodology. They have been addressing the problem in the wrong way. Moreover, we think that adequate answers *do* exist and can be identified. Our use of experiments to generate consensus on questions of distributive justice (Frohlich, Oppenheimer, and Eavey 1987a, 1987b; Frohlich and Oppenheimer 1990) has led us to conclude that the experimental laboratory provides a method for making cumulative progress in ethics. This optimism is founded in the results we have generated, but it is also based on everyday experience. After all, although it is often hard to get consensus on what is fair, it is usually easy to get agreement on what is grossly *un*fair. And that agreement can be very broad. One need

1

not be Chinese, for example, to feel outrage at characteristic abuses that took place prior to the Chinese revolution. Forcing a peasant to sell his child into bondage to purchase a bottle of aspirin for his sick wife is a practice that is not hard to identify as unfair (Hinton, 1966). Similarly, one need not have lived in the nineteenth century to feel outrage at the "gift" of blankets infested with smallpox to American Indians. The Nazi massacres of Jews and Gypsies during World War II are also likely to speak to humanity throughout its future.

The universal identifiability of the unfair is strong presumptive evidence for the existence of a common moral sense. Underlying this evidence seem to be general principles shared by people with diverse backgrounds and experiences. Indeed, this common sense of injustice may be what permits great literature to be widely appreciated. If people who lived in different times and cultures had substantially varying notions of what was unfair, it would be impossible for them to empathize with the injustices that form the basis of many classics of world literature. What was written in a distant past or place would not move diverse contemporary readers. But it does.

This asymmetry between easy agreement on *what is unfair* and lack of progress in philosophy in determining *what is fair* can shed light on how one might proceed to gain deeper insight. The examples cited are unfair because, in them, virtually no weight is given to the interests or welfare of one of the parties in the interaction. The outcomes do not reflect a reasonable balance of competing interests. In that sense, the examples are easy cases. The imbalance makes a judgment call of "unfair" straightforward. Philosophers are not generally interested in such relatively simple cases of injustice. Philosophers usually wish to identify not what is *unfair* but rather what is fair. They try to identify the *best* act or the *ideal* state of affairs. They want to characterize the maximal class of acts: the Just Acts. They wish to obtain not *some* balancing of competing claims but rather the *ideal, best,* or *fairest* balancing of these claims. The traditional philosophical methodology for dealing with justice has called for introspection and argument about these issues. We believe that this narrowly introspective approach has limited progress in the field of ethics because it has not allowed philosophers to introduce the diversity and fine details required to obtain the balance sought. For that, a broader strategy is needed.

This book is about such a strategy as applied to the question of distributive justice. Its focus is both substantive and methodological. We offer tentative conclusions about the *content* of distributive justice as well as about a *technique for discovering* that content. We argue that the key to understanding distributive justice is impartial reasoning: reasoning premised on setting aside one's particular interests and perspectives and giving balanced weight to the interests of all. It is reasoning not from one's own narrow viewpoint but from the broadest possible perspective. However, we believe that merely thinking about impartiality is not enough. An empirical approach based on laboratory experiments is required to discover what impartial individuals would do.

The line of argument leading to this conclusion begins with a set of questions: Are there theoretical conditions that generate impartial reasoning? Can these conditions produce agreement on fairness in distribution? Can we achieve, or approximate, the theoretical conditions? We offer a tentative answer to those questions and argue that it is impossible to achieve the idealized theoretical conditions. However, we do believe that they can be approximated. And our answer raises additional questions. What is the nature of the approximations? Can the approximations produce agreement about fairness in distribution? If so, what is the result? Will the agreements endure once the conditions that generated them change? What else may result from the application of a distribution rule in society? Can it have economic implications by affecting the incentives to produce? We conclude that there are empirical techniques for discovering what is fair in distribution and that those methods offer the promise of cumulative progress in the study of distributive justice.

But an empirical approach to justice must be more than a mere survey of existing beliefs. Obviously, in the everyday world, people are familiar with their own interests, and these interests color their view of what is fair. To achieve impartiality, we advocate empirical techniques that can change individuals' perspectives and aid them in a search for distributive justice. We advocate placing people in controlled laboratory conditions designed to invoke impartiality and to identify what constitutes distributive justice. Because experiments are a novel way of approaching ethical questions, a methodological discussion precedes our analysis of the substantive problem of distributive justice. In it we argue for moving ethical theorizing out of the armchair and into the laboratory.

Although this approach may appear novel, it is not without ties to recent philosophical inquiry. Much of this literature explores justice in distribution by considering conditions that could generate impartial reasoning.[1] Several philosophers have conjectured that individuals could agree on a fair pattern of distribution if they did so without knowing their own interests. John Harsanyi (1953, 1955) wondered what a group of rational, self-interested individuals would choose under such conditions. Explicitly, they were to choose from among many possible income distributions without knowing which share of the income they would get. Harsanyi argued that they would choose the distribution that maximized the group's utility. The very fact of this choice would constitute support for the principle of maximizing utility and lend it ethical standing. In *A Theory of Justice* (1971), John Rawls elaborated Harsanyi's conditions of imperfect information and asked similar questions. He, however, came to a different conclusion. Rawls argued that the group would want to maximize the utility of the worst-off individual in society.[2] He called this principle the "difference principle."

The failure of Harsanyi and Rawls to reach agreement can be

---

1. In recent literature, authors use the concept of imperfect information (borrowed from game theory) to discuss the consequences of keeping individuals in the dark about certain specific facts.

2. Rawls introduces the notion of *primary goods* and defines his principle as maximizing the primary goods available to the worst-off individual. We occasionally use the terms *welfare* or *income* as shorthand for his technical term.

attributed to a weakness in their methodology. By arguing from their individual and particular points of view, they are unable to supply the contextual richness necessary to provide the fine balance among group members' interests, and hence they cannot deduce definitive and convincing results. Group decision making is a dynamic process. Consensus requires give and take. It may be that one person simply cannot appreciate the values and life experiences of others deeply enough to understand the subtle shaping and trading of values that might take place in a group interaction. Intuiting the result of a group discussion involving diverse people may be beyond the cognitive capacity of a single individual. We argue that experimental techniques can help fill in the gaps by broadening representation and simulating the decision process.

But there are additional problems with the approach taken by Harsanyi and Rawls. The use of imperfect information by both authors led them to focus on the pattern of the resulting distribution rather than on other aspects of the problem. But other authors objected strenuously to their concentration on distributive patterns. Spearheaded by the work of Robert Nozick (1974), this literature underscores the role of property rights (or ownership), just compensation for work, and other entitlements in questions of distributing property and income. From Nozick's perspective, emphasis should be placed on fair procedures for maintaining entitlement to the rightful fruit of one's labor. In theory, a clear tension exists between these two approaches. Entitlement leads one to question the legitimacy of any requirement to redistribute well-gotten gains. In contrast, justice based on patterns may require some degree of redistribution as a minimum requirement of fairness.[3]

Noting this tension between entitlement and redistribution, theorists have voiced concern about the potential instability of any patterned principle of distributive justice. Although such a principle may appear fair when chosen without full knowledge of one's own position in the system, that same principle could

---

3. In later writings, Rawls (1985) shows his awareness of this tension.

chafe in practice when individuals begin to feel entitled to the property they have earned. For example, taxation is usually used to implement redistribution. Not surprisingly, individuals' responses to redistributive policies usually depend on their responses to the associated tax policy. Once individuals know their earnings and their tax bills, their conceptions of their own good may lead to dissatisfaction. The same individuals who thought of fairness as resulting from certain patterns of income distribution may come to make entitlement claims to secure what they perceive as their just desserts. Thus, they may well come to question the regime.

The specter of instability from policies of redistribution poses problems for modern theories of both distributive justice and governance. In practice, it has fallen to democratic processes to resolve these tensions in the choice and implementation of redistributional policies. In a democracy, the principle that the population exercises ultimate control over the government's power to tax is considered an effective safeguard against tyranny. The underlying mythology of the democratic creed holds that the process of allocating authority to the general citizenry will lead to policies that are both acceptable and fair.

But in modern, large-scale, representative democracies, the single voter exercises that authority indirectly, at a great distance, and with minimal information. Indeed, in many democracies, many voters fail to participate in the democratic process in any meaningful way. Citizens usually take taxation as it comes. Only rarely does taxation rouse citizens from their "rational ignorance" to act with consequences for the political competitors in the system.[4] Yet in their everyday lives, workers live intimately with the consequences of the taxation system. Standard economic reasoning argues that raising taxes reduces the incentives to earn and thus limits potential gains in productivity. Economic growth suffers. Ultimately, these results may even affect the acceptability of governments and the prin-

---

4. The term *rational ignorance* was first coined by Downs (1957). It refers to the small incentives an individual has to get political information, given how little difference one individual makes in the political process.

ciples of economic distribution associated with them. Hence, conceptions of justice in distribution have potentially severe economic and political consequences. They raise serious practical questions.

But little empirical work has examined the impact of particular rules of distributive justice either on productivity or on the continued acceptability of particular income-distribution policies.[5] Even fewer of these works focus on the group choice of principles of distributive justice or the stability of those choices. This book attempts to address some of these broad issues, using evidence from laboratory experiments.[6]

In Part 1 of the book we discuss the rationale for using experimental techniques in ethical theorizing and lay out the contours of the experiments. In Part 2 we address the following substantive questions explicitly. Under appropriate conditions of imperfect information:

1. Can groups generally reach unanimous decisions regarding principles of distributive justice?
2. Will groups that can reach consensus always agree on the same principle?
3. Will the consensus settle (as Rawls argued) on the difference principle—the principle that makes the worst-off individual

5. Despite the general lack of empirical work in the area, Rawls's theory has encouraged a number of efforts that examine his arguments as they bear on distributive justice. An early attempt to test one particular aspect of Rawls's argument as it relates to these questions is described in Brickman (1977). Essays in Greenberg and Cohen (1982) discuss many of the social-psychological theories, issues, and findings bearing on distributive justice, as do Bierhoff, Cohen, and Greenberg (1986) and Deutsch (1985). From different disciplinary perspectives Hochschild (1981) and Soltan (1982) present reviews of some empirical findings and tests that bear on other aspects of distributive justice. Jasso (1980, 1986), building on a tradition of equity theory in sociology, has attempted to represent sentiments regarding justice in mathematical form. More germane to the points we are concerned about here, Hoffman and Spitzer (1985) have done experiments directly testing subjects' sensitivity to entitlement as a basis for fair distribution.

6. Previous papers from this research program include Frohlich, Oppenheimer and Eavey (1987a and 1987b), Lissowski, Tyszka, and Okrasa (1991), Bond and Park (1991), and Frohlich and Oppenheimer (1989 and 1990). These articles have reported experimental tests of some of the central aspects of Rawls's argument regarding choices of principles of distributive justice.

as well off as possible? Or will groups opt for maximizing expected utility as Harsanyi argued?[7] Or will another principle emerge?

In Part 3 our concerns center on both the stability of the choice and the effects of the policies on productivity. We also explore what happens when individuals become active participants in the system of their own design.

1. Is continued acceptance of a distributive policy a function of economic experience under the policy imposed by the group?
2. Does the enforcement of the redistribution affect productivity?
3. Does democratic participation make a difference in the answers to these questions?

These are important questions, and together they constitute an ambitious agenda. Answering them requires some methodological superstructure. We therefore, at the outset, beg the reader's indulgence and patience in reading through the methodological introduction. We think it will be worth the trip—that some of the results will come as surprises, and some will have major implications.

7. In the subject handbooks Harsanyi's candidate principle was designated "maximizing the average income." It was operationalized in the income distributions as the principle that maximizes the expected monetary value to the group. In the production experiments it was operationalized as the principle that attempts to maximize the incentives for individuals to produce by allowing each participant to keep what he or she earns. There is no redistribution. In the tables and figures, for convenience, this principle will be referred to as "maximum income." When direct reference is made to the documents by the authors or by subjects, "maximizing the average" or "maximizing the average income" may be used.

PART I

Objectives, Methods, and Research Design

The project of giving to ethical life an objective and determinate grounding in considerations about human nature is not, in my view, very likely to succeed. But it is at any rate a comprehensible project, and I believe it represents the only intelligible form of ethical objectivity at the reflexive level. It is worth asking what would be involved in its succeeding. . . . If the project succeeded, it would not simply be a matter of agreement on a theory of human nature. The convergence would be partly in social and psychological science, but what would matter would be a convergence to which scientific conclusions provided only part of the means.

Williams (1985, pp. 153–154)

CHAPTER ONE

Empirical Considerations Concerning Impartial Reasoning

Where does empirical inquiry fit into a quest for a theory of distributive justice? One answer to that question is direct and simple: it stems from the role of impartial reasoning in determining rules for just distributions. Specifically, we advocate empirical work because it is difficult to determine the conclusions of impartial reasoning. To show why empirical methods might be reasonable and useful, we investigate some of the bases of moral reasoning related to our approach.

THE TRADITION OF IMPARTIAL REASONING IN ETHICAL THEORY

One hallowed tradition of ethical inquiry is the invocation of impartial reasoning as a basis for achieving moral knowledge. As far back as the first century B.C., Publius Syrus of Rome noted that when disputes arise, there is an inevitable problem of bias. His dictum was "No one should be judge in his own case."[1] The intuition here is that we are likely to assign undue weight to our own interests. To obtain impartiality, third parties, not involved, should be called on to judge. In the days

1. Maxim 545, as quoted in Bartlett (1980, p. 111).

when wool was symbolic of commerce and wealth, members of the British Parliament had to declare their financial interests in a bill being debated. Members with such interests were required to retire to the door of the Commons and sit on a wool sack. Any arguments these members might offer were presumed to be unduly colored by self-interest. Sitting on "the wool sack" made this partiality concrete.

Indeed, the most famous moral dictum, the Golden Rule (do unto others as you would have them do unto you), arguably "the common moral denominator of all the world's major religions" (Gewirth 1978, p. 133), is an application of impartiality. It calls for each of us to lend equal weight to the concerns of our fellows and even offers a simple method for invoking the requisite impartiality. "The Golden Rule is predicated upon an exchange of viewpoints, as are maxims such as that urging us to stand in another man's shoes" (Henberg 1978, p. 723).[2]

As M. C. Henberg also notes (1978, p. 723), others have sketched ways in which this impartiality might be accomplished. "C. I. Lewis, for instance, suggests that impartial valuations are best rendered by imagining that the experience of all concerned persons were one's own, . . . 'as, for example, if you had to live the lives of each of them seriatim.' Similarly, Richard Hare suggests that people who render differing moral judgements should imagine that their desires and inclinations are exchanged for the desires and inclinations of their antagonist."[3] The intuition behind these and many other similar positions is simple: to be fair, we are to project ourselves into the position of the relevant others and give equal weight to their concerns. The judgment about what is fair must be based on an impartial point of view.

2. Note that even in such technical works as those of Sen (1973, pp. 14–15) where he discusses equity his stance (which he refers to as the Weak Equity Axiom) on interpersonal comparability is not far removed from this position.
3. The internal citations are to Lewis (1946, p. 547) and Hare (1963, p. 123).

STRUCTURING AN
IMPARTIAL-REASONING DEVICE

One traditional proposal for determining the content and implications of impartiality is to adopt the perspective of an ideal observer. Such an observer would have to be endowed with certain powers to be capable of making the appropriate moral judgments. Analysis of these properties has varied, but their definition is always designed to ensure that such observers would exercise impartial reasoning in their judgments.[4] Such a proposal clearly requires that the observers have considerable knowledge plus exquisite powers of reasoning. No mere moral philosophers could claim, even in their wildest dreams, to approach these qualities even though they argue that such an ideal observer might be required to identify right principles.

Were it a straightforward matter to exercise this device to discover ethical principles, we would be making observable and indisputable progress in this area. The absence of unequivocal headway in moral theory likely reflects the difficulty of identifying and implementing a state of impartiality (in fact and principle) from which to reason. No real observer can be ideal. Real-world deviations from the idealizations of philosophers can be expected to lead to deviations in the acceptability and quality of their conclusions.

Thus, one reason for the failure to make headway in the development of theory and in the discovery of principles about justice and fairness is the inability of real people to be consistently impartial. Two clearly visible barriers are central to this failure. Individuals are unable to shed their own interests, and they have their unique perspectives, which are products of their cultural heritage, life experience, and genetic endowment. These factors inevitably lead the theorist to import biases into any attempt to reason as an impartial observer. In the end,

4. For example, Firth (1952) has specified that an ideal observer needs to be omniscient with regard to relevant nonethical facts, omnipercipient (able to empathize perfectly) with all the relevant parties, disinterested and dispassionate as among the parties and toward the issues involved, consistent (over time), as well as normal in other respects.

these shortcomings lead to ambiguity, confusion, and dispute over the fundamental issue at stake: the nature of the alternatives that would be selected. Evidence that the problem is susceptible to these difficulties includes the lack of consensus among philosophers who have used this approach to generate ethical principles. Thus, imagining an ideal observer is easier than finding one. Perhaps for this reason other proposals for identifying fair outcomes via impartial reasoning have sprung up. Some of these proposals are for devices that are disarmingly intuitive, simple, and effective. Indeed, some have been widely adopted.

Cutting Cakes

An example of a device or procedure that generates an impartial outcome is ready at hand. For two people to divide a piece of cake fairly, one person cuts and the other chooses. The principle underlying this device is elementary. The job of setting up the alternatives is separated from the job of making the choice. The general acceptability of this process is obvious. The slicer knows that any inequity between the portions is likely to work to the disadvantage of the slicer. Thus the person who is setting up the payoff structure (by slicing the cake) has every incentive to be as fair as possible in the division. So "you cut, I choose" is a universally acceptable procedural solution to the problem of two parties fairly dividing a fixed quantity.[5] This procedure has a major implication: some ethical problems have universally acceptable solutions and implementable devices for identifying them.

Although extensions of this notion to more than two persons are possible, it becomes ever more complicated as the problem of fair division becomes more complex. When the division is to be among workers who toil together to make a joint product, the procedure is inadequate, for then the quantity being divided is not fixed but is a function of the work done by

5. Some extraneous considerations such as role or status differentiation could lead the device to be rejected in particular instances.

each participant. The amount received today could be a factor determining the team member's effort tomorrow. Subtle adaptations might be required to structure a fair procedure in such complicated cases.

Imperfect Information

As mentioned in the Introduction (note 1) the device of imperfect information may be useful in dealing with complex problems of fair division. Rawls articulated a particular set of conditions of imperfect information and called them a "veil of ignorance" (1971, pp. 136–137):

> The idea . . . is to set up a fair procedure so that any principle agreed to will be just. . . . Somehow we must nullify the effects of specific contingencies which put men at odds and tempt them to exploit social and natural circumstances to their own advantage. . . . To do this I assume that the parties are situated behind a veil of ignorance. They do not know how the various alternatives will affect their own particular case and they are obliged to evaluate principles solely on the basis of general considerations.

Rawls proposed, in short, a kind of thought experiment. We are to imagine individuals (representative of classes and other social positions) deprived of all particular information about their tastes, talents, dispositions, and so forth, and asked to play the role of judge regarding rules to govern a society that they and their progeny are to inhabit. The veil prevents them from knowing the particular role they are to play in that society. This imperfect information induces conditions that generate impartial reasoning.

The conditions of Rawls (and Harsanyi) give all individuals an equal stake in every possible payoff because they do not know who they will be, and, therefore, their interest is to be fair to all. In addition to this incentive to be evenhanded, the individuals can be presumed to have the other characteristics of the ideal observer.[6] Rawls, who develops the argument more

6. Hare (1973), in his incisive review of Rawls, notes a correspondence between Rawls's veil of ignorance and ideal-observer theory. The reader can com-

fully than Harsanyi, assumes that these individuals have knowledge of the general laws governing society, can project themselves into all the possible states they might occupy, do not have any particular attachment to any given individual, and deliberate calmly until they reach a reflective equilibrium. He concludes that, as a group, such individuals would unanimously agree on a single principle.

It is possible to characterize the generic argument that lies behind this methodology of Rawls and Harsanyi. Both argue that impartial reasoning establishes the validity of a particular principle of justice. The syllogism to that effect might go as follows:

$C_1, \ldots, C_n$ are the ideal conditions of impartiality.
Any principle unanimously accepted under ideal conditions of impartiality is a valid principle of justice.
Under $C_1, \ldots, C_n$ principle P would be accepted unanimously.
Therefore P is a valid principle of justice.

Harsanyi and Rawls then use thinking about how such individuals might choose as a basis for determining a just organization of society. No doubt this device casts a powerful light on the issues at hand, but it is clearly filtered through the eyes of the beholder. So it is not surprising that they reach different conclusions about which principle will receive universal support.

The reasons for the divergence are not hard to identify. For individuals behind the veil to make judgments about principles of distributive justice, they must have at least two things: some residual preferences regarding alternative states of the world and some notions of how different choices and behavior relate to achieving preferred states.[7] These preferences can vary.

---

pare Rawls's list with Firth's (see footnote 4 above). But note that there are some significant differences (including the fact that an impartial observer would have to take into account interacting utilities) and that Rawls's and Harsanyi's derivations posit (perhaps counterfactually) that people are self-interested.

7. They must, in other words, have some knowledge of causal relationships about empirical matters.

Rawls tries to confine this variance by limiting the objects to be considered. The only explicit notions of "the good" that Rawls (1971, p. 142) allows behind the veil are "that they would prefer more primary social goods rather than less." Here Rawls (p. 92) defines primary social goods as "rights and liberties, opportunities and powers, income and wealth." Thus a rule of distributive justice is reduced to a rule for dividing primary social goods. But even a short list of primary social goods leaves open the question of potential tradeoffs between quantities of the items on the list. Even if individuals prefer, as posited, more to less, how much gain in power should be traded for how much decrease in wealth or income, and so forth? These questions are important because the agents must live with their choices.

Agents would later gain further information and occupy and judge the states they have created. That *post hoc* judgment would determine the acceptability of the decisions taken behind the veil. If application of a procedure leads to general *post hoc* dissatisfaction, the result is not likely to be stable. But how can individuals, behind a veil of ignorance, know how they will feel with their recovered tastes? In the absence of that knowledge, there is no way of specifying *ex ante* what their choices might be. Thus, two items hamper reasoning about what might be concluded under conditions of impartiality:

1. the difficulty of specifying the content of individuals' knowledge in that state
2. the difficulty of predicting the acceptability of the choices after the individual exits that state of ignorance

In other words, theorists seem unable to provide a rich enough texture for the hypothetical individuals who are making the decisions.

Thus, reasoning about what might happen under ideal conditions of impartiality is fraught with peril: the employment of the mere procedures as a guide leaves one with ambiguous conclusions. As Stephen Darwall (1983, p. 94) notes in discussing the question of the motivating power of preferences: "If we put so much distance between ourselves and the objects of our intrinsic preferences that what initially attracted us about them no longer does so at all, then we are left with no basis for choice." To the extent that Harsanyi and Rawls cannot be precise regarding those tastes that remain vested in individuals behind the veil, their conclusions are subject to biases in their projections. And any individual can conceivably be subject to some distortion of perspective when viewing the original position through the lens of his or her own experience, knowledge, and intuition. As Hare puts it, "The truth is that it is a wide open question how the POPs [people in the original position] would choose; he [Rawls] has reduced the information available to them and about them so much that it is hard to say what they would choose, unless his own intuitions supply the lack" (1973, p. 250).

It is difficult to project one's own values and expectations into situations that have consequences for others. It is even more problematic when those others have life experiences, values, and goals that we can only dimly imagine. A single philosopher, with the best of intentions, trying to find a fair rule to govern the future lives of diverse individuals can make serious miscalculations. Even the best efforts to be fair and impartial may fail because of an inability to consider properly the real perspectives and needs of others.

Thus, it should not be surprising that different views of human nature lead Harsanyi and Rawls to different conclusions about how people would choose under uncertainty. Again, Hare (1973, p. 249) puts it succinctly:

> The POP game is in effect played by imagining ourselves in the original position and then choosing principles of justice. Rawls' POPs come to the decisions that they come to simply because they are replicas of Rawls himself with what altruism he has removed and a veil of ignorance clapped over his head. It is not surprising, therefore, that they reach conclusions which he can accept.

And there is yet another source of difficulty. Although individuals are severely limited in the particular information they have, they are presumed to have certain general knowledge at their disposal. They are "presumed to know the general facts about human society. They understand political affairs and the principles of economic theory; they know the basis of social organization and the laws of human psychology" (Rawls 1971, p. 137). Alas, given the current state of knowledge in the social and behavioral sciences, it is absolutely safe to assert that there is no consensus on those laws and principles. Nor can there be any assurance that, even were a consensus to exist, those laws would point in a single "correct" direction. Thus Harsanyi and Rawls implicitly rely on unarticulated and potentially suspect scientific principles to reach their conclusions, and, being imperfect, they not surprisingly make different inferences. There is no objective way of identifying, assigning, and hence using a single set of general principles as the basis for reasoning from behind the veil. Any explicit assignment of basic knowledge is sure to be contestable; any implicit assignment, suspect.

Thus, those who argue for imperfect information as a device for promoting impartial reasoning are vulnerable to the assertion that implicit subjectivity colors their conclusions. They are insufficiently explicit about both the personal and the general knowledge held by the uninformed individuals. This lack of explicitness leaves them open to a criticism made by Thomas Nagel (1986, p. 10) in his discussion of progress in philosophy: "We also have to recognize that philosophical ideas are acutely sensitive to individual temperament, and to wishes. Where the evidence and arguments are too meager to determine a result, the slack tends to be taken up by other factors. The personal flavor and motivation of each great philosopher's version of reality is unmistakable." Thus, the deductive and introspective traditions have inherent difficulties in identifying the content of impartiality. Their attempts to strip individuals of their identity to generate impartiality are doomed to yield a vacuous version of impartiality.

We therefore propose to look elsewhere for the content of impartiality, and we suggest that empirical evidence may be generated to identify this content. This is not a great departure from the commentaries on this literature. For example, Hare has written of Rawls's theory: "Rawls does not conceive of moral philosophy as depending primarily on the analysis of valid moral argument. Rather, he thinks of a theory of justice as analogous to a theory in empirical science. It has to square with what he calls 'facts,' just like, for example, physiological theories. But what are the facts?" (1973, p. 145).[8]

THE ROLE OF EMPIRICAL METHODS

As we have seen, mere hypothesizing and reasoning about what might happen under conditions of impartiality are doomed to ambiguity. Still, a device producing conditions of imperfect information could be an acceptable generator of impartial reasoning. Although it is clearly impossible to replicate the ideal conditions of impartial reasoning, one can model and approximate them. Were we to do so, the general syllogism above would be replaced by a new one with empirical content. This content provides one possible relationship between empirical inquiry and these ethical issues.[9] We begin the new syllogism by maintaining the basic premise:

> Any principle unanimously accepted under ideal conditions of impartiality is a valid principle of justice.

and replacing the other statements as follows:

> $C_1^*, \ldots, C_n^*$ are experimental approximations to the ideal conditions of impartiality.
> Any principle unanimously agreed on under experimental conditions $C_1^*, \ldots, C_n^*$ has a claim to be a valid principle of justice.

Because we have constructed a series of experiments that attempt to approximate the ideal conditions, our claim is that:

> Any principle unanimously agreed on in our experiments has a claim as a valid principle of distributive justice.

8. See footnote 11 below, and the surrounding discussion for more on Hare's point.

9. We are indebted to Thomas Schwartz for suggesting this particular form of the argument.

Yet another, closely related, argument can be made about the rejectability of some candidates for principles of justice. Two supplementary syllogisms could be constructed parallel to the previous syllogisms. The first would be based on the following premise as a substitute for the original confirmatory ideal premise:

> Any principle incapable of getting substantial support under ideal conditions of impartiality is presumably rejectable as a valid principle of justice.

Again, because ideal conditions are not realizable, we develop a second argument by substituting empirical approximations of ideal conditions:

> $C_1^*, \ldots, C_n^*$ are experimental approximations to the ideal conditions of impartiality.
> Any principle incapable of getting substantial support under experimental conditions $C_1^*, \ldots, C_n^*$ can be presumed to be rejectable as a valid principle of justice.

And because, as stated above, we constructed experiments to approximate the ideal conditions, our claim is that:

> Those principles identified as incapable of getting substantial support under our experimental conditions can be presumed rejectable as valid principles of justice.

Together the two arguments do not quite make for necessary and sufficient conditions. Yet our claim is strong: (1) Principles that survive with unanimous support have a claim to validity as principles of justice. (2) Those that do not show any strength at all are presumably rejectable. Clearly there are big loopholes in these claims. Some aspects relevant to the analysis of distributive justice might not be properly considered, and the final determination might be mistaken. Some principles weakly affirmed or not strongly rejected might fare better under other approximations of the ideal conditions. Considerable variation in experimental conditions may be required to get a feel for the robustness of any claims.

To make these abstract arguments concrete and to generate

falsifiable conclusions, we begin with the conceptions of impartial reasoning implicit in Rawls's and Harsanyi's models of imperfect information. We develop a laboratory simulation to approximate those conditions and place subjects under those conditions to discover what they choose. This procedure shifts the grounds of the argument from the purely analytical to the empirical. This shift is justified because the central question raised by contractarian theories (such as those of Harsanyi and Rawls) is empirical. The central question is not whether a contract has ever been entered into but whether such a contract would ever be entered into under the specified conditions, and, if so, what its content would be.

There are two traditional ways of evaluating imperfect-information arguments. The first is to question the normative premises that underlie the theory. The second is to examine the validity of the logical inferences. We open a third door. We suggest empirical methods, using the syllogisms above, to illuminate what would happen under ideal conditions of impartial reasoning. After all, a key element of the theories is the presumed individual behaviors under specifiable conditions. One can test such presumptions. In other words, one can evaluate the empirical assertions of the theory.

The theories maintain that individuals would choose one or another principle. But, as shown, the arguments are not definitive. They would be compelling, as ethical arguments, only if—as the ideal conditions were empirically approximated—the choices of individuals showed, on the average, a tendency to approximate those predicted in the ideal. The conception is similar to a notion of robustness regarding scientific theories. For example, a theory of motion may be defined in the context of an ideal construct, such as a vacuum. Because a perfect vacuum is unattainable, we test the theory under less than ideal conditions. Bridge concepts and supplementary theories about the impact of imperfections in conditions permit an evaluation of the theory in the real world.

As the ideal is approached, the predictions must increase in accuracy or the theory becomes uninteresting. Failure to exhibit this sort of robustness would constitute a vulnerability or brittleness that would deprive the theory of a considerable degree of attractiveness.[10] If one or another theoretical conclusion does not bear out as the conditions are approximated, the weight we ought to give it diminishes. This is so in science, and we believe it should be so with theories of distributive justice.

There are yet other advantages to using actual experiments. Conducted as thought experiments, the arguments of Harsanyi and Rawls invoke the considered judgment of only one observer from the perspective of his or her experience.[11] As a real experiment with approximated conditions one can have a selection of participants representing a variety of perspectives and cultures. Testing of this sort also opens the possibility of a wide sampling of the subjective components (for example, relevant knowledge and preference) that are so difficult to identify precisely a priori. In addition, experiments force the subjects to focus on the issue of justice in a direct fashion. And how much better it is to have them contemplating a real (rather than an abstract) decision with concrete implications to concentrate their minds. As Jonathan Harrison notes in commenting on Roderick Firth's notion of an ideal observer: "We do not verify ethical statements by observing the reactions of ideal observers, for either there are none, or we do not have the opportunity

10. Findings in chaos theory imply that we might not expect uniform increased accuracy in the predictions of the idealized theory as the ideal conditions were approached. Wild gyrations might well occur. Nevertheless, a reasonably wide sampling of instances as the ideal was approached should still reveal some central tendencies. Purely random results or results totally at variance with the predictions of the theory are not to be expected. Were they found, the accuracy of the theory would truly be questionable.

11. We say only one observer, but Hare says two: the reader and the author. Return to the quote from Hare at the end of the previous section. We ended that quote with Hare's question "But what are the facts?" Hare continues, a few lines later, "Rawls, in short, is here advocating a kind of subjectivism, in the narrowest and most old-fashioned sense. He is making the answer to the question 'Am I right in what I say about moral questions?' depend on the answer to the question 'Do you the reader, and I agree in what we say?' This must be his view, if the considered judgements of author and reader are to occupy the place in his theory which is occupied in an empirical science by the facts of observation. Yet . . . he claims objectivity for his principles" (1973, p. 145).

of observing them. Statements about the reactions of ideal observers would, presumably, be verified by observing the ideal reactions of actual observers" (1956, p. 259).

To those who would object to, or challenge, our conclusions, the following questions could serve as likely jumping off points:

1. Are $C_1, \ldots, C_n$ the conditions of impartiality?
2. Are $C_1{}^*, \ldots, C_n^*$ reasonable enough approximations of $C_1, \ldots, C_n$ to serve as an environment for an initial test of the theory?

But objections to the enterprise on the basis that the ideal has not been attained cannot be accepted. After all, the notion of robustness, or approximation of the ideal, as a basis for gaining leverage has a long tradition in political philosophy. It goes back at least as far as Plato. In discussing the ideal state in his *Republic*, Plato (p. 178) notes that the purely ideal state is unattainable but also that this fact should not prevent one from attempting to approximate it as closely as possible:

> Can theory ever be fully realized in practice? (He answers 'No'.) . . . Then you must not insist upon my showing that this construction we have traced in thought could be reproduced in fact down to the last detail. You must admit that we shall have found a way to meet your demand for realization, if we can discover how a state might be constituted in the closest accordance with our description. Will that not content you? It would be enough for me.

Or, to put it differently, because an argument is an idealization does not mean that it is without empirical content. Indeed, one could argue that only insofar as (political) ethics has an empirical element is it appreciably differentiated from logic and mathematics. Thus our interest here is not in what some have called the geometry of morals but in the physics of morals.

CHAPTER TWO

Research Problems

Our major research questions can be broken into two sets. The first deals with the results of the impartial-reasoning process:

1. Can individuals reach unanimous agreement on a principle of distributive justice under conditions of impartiality?
2. Will different groups under the same conditions always choose the same principle?
3. Will they choose the difference principle, as posited by Rawls, or to maximize expected utility, as argued by Harsanyi, or some other principle?

The second set of questions focuses on the acceptability of a given principle when the subjects experience the principle in practice.[1]

1. Is the continued acceptability of a principle a function of economic experience under the policy imposed by that principle?
2. Is productivity affected by experiencing the redistribution required by that principle?
3. Are there differences in the answers to the two preceding questions when the principle is imposed rather than agreed on in a participatory fashion?

1. In our experiments, and in theory, this experience would occur after the conditions used to generate impartial reasoning have been removed.

Our general procedure for answering such questions has been sketched. In the laboratory, we approximate conditions of impartial reasoning and ask individuals to decide on a principle for dividing payoffs. They lack knowledge regarding which share they will receive. Their ignorance is intended to induce impartial reasoning, and it is hoped that they will choose a principle from that vantage point. This notion lies at the heart of justice-as-fair-division arguments.

Rawls and Harsanyi construct their arguments from numerous assumptions. For example, they assume that the individuals involved are rational and self-interested (the traditional behavioral assumptions of microeconomics). Rawls further posits that individuals are almost exclusively concerned with the possibility that they may be among the worst off.[2] Harsanyi, by contrast, assumes that people are expected-value maximizers. In our experimental situation we cannot posit behavior but rely, instead, on the revealed behavior of real human beings in the laboratory.

CONDITIONS FOR CHOOSING A PRINCIPLE

But choices cannot be made in a vacuum. Institutional conditions and constraints must be specified. As Hare says (1973, p. 149):

> The important thing to notice about all such [hypothetical-choice] theories is that what this hypothetical person would choose, if it is determinate at all (which many such theories fail to make it) has to be determined by the conditions to which he is subject. If the conditions once made explicit, do not deductively determine the choice, then the choice remains indetermi-

2. Rawls's formulation of the difference principle is related to the psychological models, or behavioral assumptions, that underlie game theory. Von Neumann and Morgenstern (1948) postulated that when faced with choices under uncertainty (where there is no information regarding the probabilities of relevant outcomes), individuals choose to maximize their "security level." According to Rawls (1971, pp. 154–155) this hypothesis of "floor maximizing" is the appropriate one to describe behavior in the original position.

nate, except in so far as it is covertly conditioned by the prejudices or intuitions of the philosophers whose theory it is.

What is the context of the deliberations and choice in the laboratory? Our experimental conditions parallel those set up by Rawls in his indeterminate thought experiment. An enumeration of his conditions serves as a guide to our design and his intentions. Rawls structures the situation carefully to generate his conclusions. He posits: the stakes involved in the distributive issue; the restricted level of information available to the individuals; the agenda of principles of distributive justice; and the procedures for discussion of, and voting on, the most preferred principle.

Rawls (as well as Harsanyi) assumes that the stakes involved are high: one's life chances and the life chances of one's descendants. The only restriction on the range of the stakes is Rawls's proviso that the society in question is to be one of "moderate scarcity." Clearly, our experimental conditions must fall far short of these stakes.

For Rawls and Harsanyi, the restriction on information (the veil of ignorance) is used to induce impartial reasoning among the individuals. Individuals cannot know their talents, skills, tastes, or statuses in the society for which they are making a decision. Nor can the individuals have specific information regarding the nature of that society beyond the knowledge that it is one of moderate scarcity (Rawls 1971, pp. 18–19, 136–142). Moreover, the individuals are assumed to come to the original position without preconceptions as to what constitutes social welfare, fairness, or "the good."[3] In our experimental situation, subjects are unaware of the position they will occupy after a decision is made, but they must retain all their other information and knowledge. Thus they bring a broad range of experi-

---

3. As noted in Chapter 1 the theories developed are insufficiently explicit about what remains in the minds of the individuals to allow for a rigorous deduction of their conclusions. This inability to specify the residual content of values and knowledge behind a veil of ignorance is the Achilles heel of the pure theorist.

ences and values to bear. Because they are ignorant of their ultimate position, however, they retain the critical incentive to be fair to all.[4]

As to agenda and procedures, we follow Rawls as closely as possible. He specifies (1971, p. 124) the principles of distributive justice that should be considered. Individuals are charged with discussing principles that maximize the primary social goods of the worst-off individual in the society, maximize the total utility in the society, or maximize the average utility in the society (these last two are identical if societal size is fixed because the option of changing utility levels by increasing or decreasing the population is not available); he also specifies a variety of mixed principles. Rawls insists that the decision be preceded by an extensive, open discussion in which the merits of the principles are considered. Furthermore, the decision is to be reached in a "consensus reaching style." Individuals are to continue discussions until they feel comfortable with their decisions. Only after they have exhausted their arguments and reached a "reflective equilibrium" is a formal decision to be reached. The rule for reaching agreement is unanimity.

CONSENSUS ON DISTRIBUTIVE JUSTICE

Under these conditions, we seek to answer the first three questions listed at the beginning of this chapter. Our conjectures differ from those of both Rawls and Harsanyi. We believe that individual evaluations of choices are richer than a narrow-minded focus on the worst outcome and that they take into account other elements. Moreover, our conjecture regarding the choice of principles by individuals is consistent with a theoretical result of Roger Howe and John Roemer (1981). They

---

4. It could be, however, that expectations regarding success are engendered by family and social history and could distort notions of fairness by making our veil less meaningful. If that were the case, the socioeconomic characteristics of the subjects would be strong factors in determining the individual decisions in our laboratories. This is an avenue we explore in detail in the forthcoming chapters.

modeled the problem of a choice of a distributive principle behind the veil of ignorance as a game and concluded that the choice of distributive principle would be a function of the degree of risk aversion among the individuals. One implication of their analysis is that if the individuals choosing a principle exhibit a moderate degree of risk aversion, there will be an identifiable core of the choice game.[5] The core would consist of the mixed principle of setting a floor (funded presumably via the necessary tax) and otherwise allowing incomes to be unconstrained. The subsequent diversity of income potential would allow for the (constrained) maximization of group income. Whereas Rawls assumed a high degree of risk aversion, Harsanyi assumed risk neutrality.[6] But because populations of individuals have a variety of risk propensities and expectations, both theoretical and empirical reasons lead one to believe that the principle most likely to be chosen would be a mixed principle.

In previous experiments conducted in different contexts (Miller and Oppenheimer 1982; Eavey and Miller 1984; and Frohlich and Oppenheimer 1984), we observed individuals attempting to take into account the cardinal properties of the rewards that they, as a group, could gain as a result of any distributive principle. Other experimenters have also found that group decisions about distribution deal with more aspects of the distribution than were posited by either Harsanyi or Rawls (Brickman 1977; Hoffman and Spitzer 1985; and Marwell and Ames 1979, 1980). For these reasons, we conjecture that individuals would neither choose simply to maximize the primary social goods of the worst-off individual nor opt to maximize expected value. Rather, they would wish to take into account

5. The core consists of those outcomes where no group of players find they can guarantee themselves an improvement by forming a coalition to get a different outcome. Therefore, if an outcome of a social interaction is not in a core, some coalition can be sure of doing better if it forms to change the outcome. Hence, outcomes not in a core might be considered unstable.

6. Another interpretation of Harsanyi's position has been suggested to us by Dennis Mueller. He points out that if an equiprobable estimate of life chances is made by the individuals, then they will wish to maximize expected value.

additional attributes of the situation. The needs of individuals unable to care for themselves, entitlements to the fruits of one's labors, and the economic need for incentives for productivity would all enter into their deliberations. They would also be concerned with the tradeoffs among the floor, the ceiling, the mean, and so forth. Thus, we expect the group decision to center around tradeoffs between competing attributes of different income distributions, for even in the austerity of laboratory situations individuals are faced with tradeoffs similar to those faced when making any economic decision.

In sum, we can expect a considerable degree of consensus, perhaps even unanimity, but we predict results that conform to the predictions of neither Harsanyi nor Rawls. We expect an outcome less egalitarian than the difference principle, one that takes the welfare of the poor as only one aspect among many. The reward of those who work hard and are productive will not be ignored.

Specifically, we believe that individuals exercising impartial reasoning will choose a compound principle, referred to by Rawls as "intuitionistic principle(s) of justice" or "mixed conceptions of justice" (1971, pp. 34–40, 316). They permit a weighing of values to reflect a complex notion of justice. Two such principles are explicitly considered (and rejected) by Rawls; each constrains the principle which maximizes the average utility.[7] The first constrains it by placing a limit on the acceptable range of incomes in the society.[8] The difference between the best- and worst-off members of society is not to exceed a given amount. The second constrains it by imposing a guaranteed floor, or minimum income below which no one can fall.

To test these competing views, we have created conditions

7. We will henceforth use the term *income* as a substitute for the more cumbersome *primary social goods* when we refer to principles of distributive justice. This choice, in part, is more than semantic. It should remind the reader of a limitation in our experiments: they necessarily exclude from consideration such primary social goods as rights and concentrate only on material goods.

8. The range of incomes is the distance (in this case monetary) between the highest and lowest incomes in the society.

in our experiments that are designed to generate impartial reasoning. To the extent that these experiments are an approximate empirical realization of the ideal conditions of impartiality, they constitute a method for casting light on questions of distributive justice.

IMPLEMENTATION AND STABILITY

But the achievement of a consensus and the identification of its content are just the beginning. If any such consensus is to be meaningful, it must stand the test of practice. The acceptability of a principle must not disintegrate once it is adopted as social policy. In other words one must ask, "Is it stable?"[9] If it is not stable, the principle may not be implementable or, even if implementable, may engender unanticipated and unacceptable consequences when put into practice. Clearly there is a potential conflict between the ex ante choice and subsequent stability. This conflict will be reflected in the political fabric of the community after the distributive rights are agreed on.

For example, imagine a principle were agreed on and implemented as part of a social contract. If it resulted either in a significant diminution of productivity or in a significant alienation of some of those living under the policy, those consequences could threaten the stability of the political system. Such threats would make the achievement of an ex ante consensus behind the veil a less than compelling result. Therefore, we must explore the effects of the principle on the subsequent behavior of subjects. This concern is reflected in the second list of questions at the beginning of this chapter.

Here again, Rawls's work acts as a guide. He is aware that part of the problem of justice is political, and he identifies two characteristics of people that must be taken into account in any theory. These characteristics are the capacity for individual welfare ("the capacity for a conception of the good") and the

9. A number of papers could be cited to indicate opposing thoughts on these matters. Most germane to our discussion are the works of Nozick (1974) and Rawls (1985).

capacity for social welfare ("the capacity for a sense of justice")
(1985, p. 237):

1. "A conception of the good is the capacity to form, to revise, and rationally to pursue a conception of one's rational advantage or good."
2. "A sense of justice is the capacity to understand, to apply, and to act from the public conception of justice which characterizes the fair terms of social cooperation."

Both aspects must be taken into account in any policy concerning distribution. A central problem for a theory of distributive justice is the size of the gap between these two aspects after a choice has been made from a position of impartiality. A viable solution to the distributive problem must provide the basis for bridging that gap politically.

In the next chapter, we sketch our research design for finding a principle of distributive justice that is stable. In subsequent parts of the book, we provide tentative, empirical answers to the questions we have posed at the beginning of this chapter.

CHAPTER THREE

Research Design

Our research is guided by two assumptions: impartiality holds the key to distributive justice, and imperfect information, of a particular kind, generates impartiality. Experimental subjects are confronted with a laboratory situation in which they are ignorant of their own self-interest. Under these conditions they, as a group, choose a principle of distributive justice to govern their rewards. To ensure that our experimental design did not rig the results, we checked to see how sensitive the results were to the specific experimental conditions. Moderate changes in the design should not have produced radically different results. To ensure against cultural bias, and hence nongeneralizability of the results, we sampled more than one national and cultural population. The various experimental conditions are displayed in Table 1, which also indicates where the different variants of the experiment were run. These variations are explained in this chapter.

BASIC EXPERIMENTAL DESIGN

The first tier of experiments (five varieties) was designed to test choices of principles of distributive justice under approximate conditions of impartiality. Though not perfectly similar to the

Table 1. Variations of Experimental Conditions.

	Regular Stakes with Distribution of		High Stakes with Distribution of	
	Gains	Losses	Gains	Losses
Experiments without Production				
Justice	**	*	*	*
Nonjustice	+			
Experiments with Production[a]				
Unanimity	+			
Majority Rule	+			
Imposed	+			

** Run in Poland, Canada & 2 U.S. Sites
 * Run in 2 U.S. Sites and Canada
 + Run in Maryland only
[a] All the production experiments involved gains and used the handbooks with explicit references to justice

constructs in the philosophical discussions, they were designed to help us examine the validity of the empirical assumptions at the core of the normative debate. We attempted to determine which principles of distributive justice, if any, subjects would agree on. To appreciate the content and thrust of the experiments, it is useful to follow the broad outlines of the process experienced by the subjects. Details of the experiments are discussed later in this chapter.

For each group we solicited, as subjects, five students from university classrooms. We then escorted them to a room where the experiment was to be conducted. When the subjects were seated (each at his or her own desk), we greeted them and presented each of them with a booklet to read. The booklet began with a brief sketch of four specific principles: Rawls's difference principle, characterized as maximizing the floor income; Harsanyi's idea, depicted as maximizing the average income; and two mixed principles that were discussed in the previous chapter—constraining the average income by setting a floor or a range.[1] Although our immediate goal was to ensure that the subjects understood the principles, it was important that we not bias them by our description of the problem. So we simply sketched the principles as follows:

> To illustrate such principles consider the following four notions of justice:
>
> 1.   MAXIMIZING THE FLOOR INCOME
>
> *The most just distribution of income is that which maximizes the floor (or lowest) income in the society.*
> This principle *considers only the welfare of the worst-off individual in society.* In judging among income distributions, *the distribution which ensures the poorest person the highest income is the most just.* No person's income can go up unless it increases the income of the people at the very bottom.
>
> 2.   MAXIMIZING THE AVERAGE INCOME
>
> *The most just distribution of income is that which maximizes the average income in the society.*

---

1. As indicated in Table 1, we had a variation of the experiment in which the notion of justice was downplayed. In those experiments certain replacements were made in the booklet. These included, for example, substituting "rules for distributing the monetary gains and losses" for "principles of justice." Given the fixed size of the group (five subjects), some principles become redundant. For example, under these circumstances, maximizing the average income is the same as maximizing total income.

For any society maximizing the average income maximizes the total income in the society.

3. MAXIMIZING THE AVERAGE WITH A FLOOR CONSTRAINT OF $_____

The most just distribution of income is that which maximizes the average income only after a certain specified minimum income is guaranteed to everyone.

Such a principle ensures that the attempt to maximize the average is constrained so as to ensure that individuals "at the bottom" receive a specified minimum. To choose this principle one must specify the value of the floor (lowest income).

4. MAXIMIZING THE AVERAGE WITH A RANGE CONSTRAINT OF $_____

The most just distribution of income is that which attempts to maximize the average income only after guaranteeing that the difference between the poorest and the richest individuals (i.e., the range of income) in the society is not greater than a specified amount.

Such a principle ensures that the attempt to maximize the average does not allow income differences between rich and poor to exceed a specified amount. To choose this principle one must specify the dollar difference between the high and low incomes.

Of course, there *are* other possible principles, and you may think of some of them.

After this minimal introduction to the principles, we asked subjects to rank the principles and to indicate how secure they felt about that ranking. Then we gave them a bit more detail about the problem they were to face by having them do a sample problem (see Table 2). The problem involved four possible patterns of income distribution, each of which had five income classes. (The average income was not given to the subjects at this point to draw their attention to the need for information on the population distribution across income classes.)

The subjects were then led through the consequences of applying each of the four principles. They were reminded both that their choice would (later) govern their payoffs and that they could not be sure which income class they would actually be in:

In making this choice, recall that your choice will yield you a payoff. How will your choice determine your pay? If, for example, you choose (a) to maximize the floor or low income, you will have picked that distribution (from the four in the sample question) which has the highest floor. (In this case distribution 4.) This ensures that you would get at least $15,000 if you were to be the worst-off individual. This is the most that a member of the low-income class could get from any of these distributions.

Subjects then read more about the principles of justice that we had placed on their (otherwise open) agenda. After all, we could not presume they had a feel for such things as the average income and how that might relate to the "height" of the minimum income. They then took a short test about various aspects of these principles. If they did not pass the test, they were required to retake a second variant of the test. Passing the test was a precondition to continuing in the experiment.[2] After the test, subjects were again polled to reveal their rankings of the four principles.

After revealing their rankings of the principles, the subjects continued to explore the nature and implications of the principles, this time experientially. In this section of the experiment, they earned money by making choices in four situations like the one presented in Table 2 (with the average incomes specified). Each subject chose from among the four principles, and each of their choices led to the selection of an income distribution. Subjects knew that they would be randomly assigned to an income class within the distribution they had chosen.[3] These assignments were made by having the subject reach into a bag and pull out a chit (see Table 3), which showed two things: their income-class assignment (and hence their payoff) and also what they would have received under each of the other

2. Individuals often failed the first time, but subsequent failures were not frequent. We helped those with difficulties by answering questions about the principles they showed evidence of misunderstanding in the test.

3. In part because of time constraints, in the experiments involving production (explained later in this chapter), this part of the experiment was excised. Also note that in the production experiments income was tied to work and not just assignment to income class.

Table 2. Sample Choice Problem

Consider the following four income distributions (each of the money entries represents a yearly dollar income for a household):

	Income Distributions			
Income Class	*1*	*2*	*3*	*4*
High	$32,000	$28,000	$31,000	$21,000
Medium high	27,000	22,000	24,000	20,000
Medium	24,000	20,000	21,000	19,000
Medium low	13,000	17,000	16,000	16,000
Low	12,000	13,000	14,000	15,000
Average income				
Floor or low income	12,000	13,000	14,000	15,000
Range	20,000	15,000	17,000	6,000

You are to make a choice from among the four principles of justice which are mentioned above: (a) maximizing the floor, (b) maximizing the average, (c) maximizing the average with a floor constraint, and (d) maximizing the average with a range constraint. If you choose (c) or (d), you will have to tell us what that floor or range constraint is before you can be said to have made a well defined choice. Your choice of a principle will select one of the four income distributions as the most just. ... Indicate your choice of a principle here: _____.

---

principles had they chosen it.[4] Thus they were familiarized not only with the implications of their particular choice but also with the consequences of different choices. Real monetary pay-offs were calculated as $1 for every $10,000 of family income shown in the tables. The amount of money subjects were to

4. The students were not able to discern the distribution of chits in the bags. Each time the subjects kept the chits so that they could reflect on the consequences of their choices. Judging from the discussions later in the experiment, this procedure had considerable pedagogic impact.

Table 3. Example of an Income Class Assignment Chit

This assigns you to the following income class:

LOW (in Situation A)

For each principle of justice the following income would be received by each member of this income class. You will receive a payoff of $1 for each $10,000 of income.

Principle of Justice	Income	Payoff
Maximizing the floor	$13,000	$1.30
Maximizing the average	6,000	0.60
Maximizing the average with a floor constraint of $12,000	12,000	1.20
Maximizing the average with a floor constraint of $10,000	10,000	1.00
Maximizing the average with a range constraint of $25,000	6,000	0.60
Maximizing the average with a range constraint of $16,000	12,000	1.20

receive was entered on their payoff sheet after each selection in order to make the payoff concrete. The idea here was to get them to experience the consequences of their choices of principles. After the four choices were made, subjects were again polled regarding their rankings of the principles.

Subjects then proceeded to the second part of the experiment. It involved a collective, or group, choice of principle. In that part they were given a chance to decide together, after a discussion, on a principle of justice.[5] Again (in the nonproduction experiments), the fact that they would be randomly assigned to an income class was emphasized. The subjects were informed that there was a set of payoff vectors, each consisting of five income classes. The vectors would be used to determine the final payoffs to the subjects.[6] However, they knew neither the number nor the content of these vectors. If they reached unanimous agreement on a principle, the chosen principle would be used to filter the payoff vectors available. For example, if they chose maximum income only the subset of vectors corresponding to that principle would be used for the drawing of a payoff vector (that is, only the payoff vectors with the highest average income would be drawn from). The payoff for each individual would be determined by random assignment to an income class within the vector drawn. If the group did not reach unanimous agreement, the schedule of payments that would be made to them would be chosen randomly from the full set of vectors (again with individual assignment to a class done randomly). As we put it:

> Your payoffs in this section of the experiment will conform to the principle which you, as a group, adopt. If you, as a group, do not adopt any principle, then we will select one of the income distributions at random for you as a group. That choice of income distribution will conform to no particular characteristics.

This procedure provided the incentive to reach an agreement. If the subjects wished to ensure that their payoffs had desirable distributional properties, they had to agree unanimously on a single principle of distributive justice. The stakes for agreement were only their being guaranteed a payoff vector that they all agreed was fair.

5. In the experiments where a principle was "imposed" on the group, the members of the group did not collectively discuss which principle they would prefer.
6. Payoff vectors were not drawn in the production experiments. There, the subjects were told that the income they earned individually would be (potentially) redistributed in accordance with the principle they chose.

We attempted in this part of the experiment to drive two other points home:

1. The distributions may not resemble the distributions in the first part.
2. The stakes in this part of the experiment are much higher than in the first part.

The first of these points was designed to ensure that subjects did not project from the sample distributions in the first part of the experiment to the second part. The second point was designed to emphasize the seriousness of the task in relation to their monetary stakes.

We permitted lengthy and open discussion.[7] Indeed, we required that unanimous agreement on secret ballots be reached to terminate discussion.[8] The agenda was open. As we put it: "You *are not restricted*, in any way, *to the four principles of justice* mentioned above. Thus, you can discuss (and later adopt) other principles. Any one of you can introduce and begin discussion of any principle." If all subjects agreed verbally that the discussion had run its course and no further discussion promised to be fruitful, a secret ballot was taken on terminating the discussion. If even a single subject felt further discussion was required, then it was resumed. If the ballot showed that all agreed that no more discussion was needed, voting on the principles was undertaken. A set of (pairwise) secret ballots was then held between all the principles on the agenda to see whether there was a unanimous choice. If there was, the players were paid off as discussed above. If no winner emerged, discussion resumed.

After the discussion and choice, subjects were asked to provide demographic, sociological, and psychological data for analysis. During the questioning, they also gave us, one last

7. A bare minimum of five minutes was required, but much longer discussions always took place. The transcripts of the discussions average more than ten single-spaced typed pages apiece.
8. This requirement, again, was varied in some of the production experiments where majoritarian procedures were used to see whether they led to differences.

time, their ranked preferences for the principles. In total, throughout the course of the experiment subjects were asked (on four different occasions) to indicate their ranking of the four principles and to indicate the degree of confidence they attached to their rankings.[9]

A summary outline of the flow of the experiment might be useful here.

In Part I we handed out a booklet that introduced subjects to the content of the experiment—the substance of the choices they were to make. This part consisted of the following steps:

1. A brief presentation of four of the principles of justice that Rawls insists must be on the agenda.

2. A preliminary ranking of the principles by the subjects.

3. A relatively long and illustrated discussion of the principles, their implications, and how the subjects' tasks related to these principles.

4. A test, to ensure us that they understood these basics.

5. A second ranking of the principles.

6. A set of four choice situations, where the subjects' choices of particular principles of justice had financial consequences for them personally. These situations involved more than reading and writing; in them the subjects randomly selected a chit that assigned them to an income class.

7. A third ranking of the principles.

In Part II the subjects participated in a collective decision under conditions of impartiality in an approximation of Rawls's original position. This part consisted of these steps:

1. Reading and clarifying instructions concerning the group discussion and choice of principle.

2. A group discussion about the choice the group was to make. This was usually a lengthy discussion. The average length was about twenty-five minutes.

3. A motion to end the discussion. This motion came strictly from the subjects themselves.

9. They were asked an additional three times in the production experiments.

4. Two unanimous agreements—first verbal and then by secret ballot—to end discussion or, failing agreement to terminate discussion, continued discussion until agreement was reached to terminate discussion.

5. A specification of the precise agenda for the vote.

6. Voting on the items on the agenda, which resulted in one of three outcomes:

    a. Unanimous agreement on a single principle resulting in termination and payment according to the group's unanimous choice (or, if anyone so wished)

    b. Recommencement of discussion (return to step 2 above) (or)

    c. Termination with payment not in conformity with any principle.

7. This voting phase was concluded when:

    a. Unanimous agreement was reached (or)

    b. The group agreed that unanimity was impossible (or)

    c. Time ran out.[10]

In cases b and c, payment was made by random selection of a payoff vector and not in conformity with any particular principle.

Part III involved administration of a debriefing questionnaire dealing with the subject's attitudes, background, and political beliefs. It also dealt with the subject's relationship to the experimental structure itself and asked the subjects for a final ranking of the principles.

VARIANTS OF THE BASIC EXPERIMENTAL DESIGN

To explore the robustness of our results, we varied the experimental conditions (see Table 1). We wanted to ensure that our results would not be a function of the peculiarities and idiosyncracies of the experimental design. For example, consider the

10. This last choice was not a part of the conceived design. However, an error in the translation of the design into Polish led to the imposition of a time constraint in the discussion periods of some of those experiments.

size of the stakes involved. Rawls and Harsanyi were arguing about principles that would govern the distributive choice of lifetime incomes for oneself, one's class, and one's offspring. Although we framed the questions and choices in similar terms, no amount of verbiage could convert the actual payoffs to choices about lifetime wages. But we could alter the size of the stakes, within the range permitted by the budget of the laboratory experiments, to see whether such alteration made any difference. If choices could be shown to vary as we varied the stakes, then the importance of our small stakes would be clear. Thus, if higher stakes changed the choice, and presumably the underlying reasoning, our experiments probably did not constitute a good test of the theories.

To check for this possible objection, we introduced two experimental variables that might be expected to affect subjects' choices: higher variances in potential payoffs (in the choice situations) and prepayment of $40 with subsequent choices leading to reductions from that credit. The results of these variations were contrasted with the results in the original, or baseline, experiments to yield an indication of the robustness of the results within the range of variation available to the experimenters. The way in which these changes in design might be expected to affect subjects' choices can be outlined simply.

Choices with Higher-Variance Payoffs

Individual choices are often a function of the framing of the situation (Tversky and Kahneman, 1981). We wanted to ensure that our results were not determined by irrelevant framing effects. One way to reframe our experiment was to make the stakes appear higher for the players. We did this by altering the income distributions in Part I so that the floors were lower, and nastier, while the ceilings were higher. This alteration raised the variance in the payoffs that subjects received when they selected principles. We conjectured that the higher variances would give them increased reason to focus on the floor as an undesirable outcome and therefore to choose to maximize the floor. If, as Rawls argues, rational individuals consider nothing but the floor when selecting a principle of justice, this depression of the available floor should have been an additional inducement to choose the highest floor. Of course the absolute value of the payoffs would still have fallen far short of "life chances," but to the extent that subjects considered the possibilities seriously, the reframing might have worked to increase the attractiveness of a principle that maximizes floor income.

Choices Involving Losses

Increasing variances by lowering the floors and raising the ceilings in Part I of our experiment was not the only way to reframe the situation for our subjects. A. Tversky and D. Kahneman (1981) contend that, for individuals, "the response to losses is more extreme than the response to gains" (p. 454). Therefore, we conjectured that if individuals were concerned with a loss, they would focus their attention on the floor. This focus would, presumably, increase the probability of choosing a principle that guaranteed a maximum floor.[11] To induce this effect we changed the design slightly by giving subjects a $40 credit prior to the second part of the experiment. In this variant they were told that their choice of a redistributive principle would determine the distribution of reductions to that $40 credit. To make the $40 credit credible, the amount was written on each subject's payoff sheet. This sheet was a cashable credit slip and was the record of the individual's earnings. Thus, subjects were choosing how to distribute losses from each of their $40 credits. Presumably, this change raised the stakes in the eyes of the participants. But this raise was purely subjective. Individuals were given reason to believe that they could win $40 in Part II (and in fact they could), but the final returns that were available to them were identical to those available to subjects in the

11. The reader should note that the results reported for this variation of the experiment are not congruent with this interpretation of Tversky and Kahneman's hypothesis. A second interpretation of their argument would be that giving subjects a credit of $40 should lead them to increase risk taking to avoid a loss in the second part of the experiment. Hence it could favor the choice of maximum income.

other variants of the experiment. This variation was run with both the original and the higher-variance payoffs.

Choices without Reference to Justice

One concern expressed by early critics of our basic research design was that explicit discussions of distributive justice in the research instrument might skew subjects' responses and choices. The argument was advanced that the subjects' desire to please the experimenters might lead them to give undue and unrealistic consideration to matters of fairness when they considered their choices impartially. Thus, their expressed preferences might unduly reflect the normative content of the research instrument. This outcome would be particularly problematic if Harsanyi and Rawls base their arguments on explicit rationality and self-interest, and make no assumption that normative arguments would be employed from an impartial point of view.

To test for this sort of bias in our basic experimental protocol, we ran one set of experiments in which all explicit references to justice were removed. Thus at the outset the subjects were told: "This experiment deals with the question of the distribution of monetary gains or losses among members of committees." Similar changes were made to remove all explicit references to justice throughout the experiment. Where the word *principles* was used in the basic experiments, the word *rules* was substituted to deemphasize the normative content. One can get a sense of the contrast from a quick description at the start of Part I of the experiments. Regular version: "This experiment is concerned with the justice of different income distributions. Let us begin by discussing some ways of judging the justice of an income distribution." Nonjustice version: "This experiment is concerned with committee decisions about rules to distribute income among members of a society which *includes you.* Let us begin by discussing the effect of different rules on what you will get in the experiment."

In all other respects the research instrument was identical to the basic design. These changes allowed us to test the conjecture that references to justice might bias the outcome and helped ensure that any results obtained were not disproportionately reflective of secondary aspects of the experimental design.

Postchoice Stability of the Chosen Distributive Principle

Recall, we are concerned not only with the choices of principles but also with the stability of the choices after they are implemented. To test for stability, we created an experimental setting in which subjects experienced the consequences of their choice of distributive principle. We believe the stability of a redistributive policy is a function of both its redistributional impact and its effect on productivity. To test this hypothesis we needed to include a provision for production, earning, and redistribution. Furthermore, we hypothesize that the acceptability of a principle is a function of democratic participation in its choice. To test this hypothesis required that we vary the level of participation in the selection of principle.

We ran three additional sets of experiments to deal with the issues of participation and production. Again, we followed the basic research design, but we added one major component. The additional section involved the opportunity for subjects to perform a task, earn income, and then see it redistributed among group members. The research instrument was expanded to deal with taxation policies associated with each principle, so that subjects would appreciate the taxation consequences of their choices. After the principle was established, group members corrected spelling mistakes in texts excerpted from the works of Talcott Parsons. Each text was arduous (as the reader can easily confirm by reading any random selection from Parsons or by examining the sample paragraph from one of our tasks in Table 4) and contained about twenty spelling errors.

Each individual performed the same task, and each received wages for his or her individual production. The marginal pay rate had considerable returns to scale as is apparent in Table 5. Outputs of each individual were checked; and their earnings,

Table 4. Sample from a Spelling-Correction Task

Let us now approach another exceadingly* important aspec* of this body of theory which relates to but goes beyond these main traditions. The emphasis on the importance of normative references as defining the situation for motivated and meaningful action has been noted. On the one hand, Weber, with reference to the cultural level, and Durkhem* to the social, then came to the important conception of common normative elements, especially beliefs and values for Weber and the conscience colective* for Durkheim. From these starting points it has gradually come to be understood that what I have called institusionalization* and internalization (with reference to personality of the individual) of these normative elements constitute the primary focus of the control of action in social systems, threw* processes whose general nature has come to be much better understood in recent years than preaviously*.

* flags the errors

taxes, and take-home pay were calculated and reported to them along with the equivalent yearly income flows implied by the earnings (see the last column in Table 5). Then their posttax payments for that period were calculated and reported to each of them. Taxes needed to raise individual incomes in accordance with the principle were assessed proportionately against the earnings of those who did not need income transfers. Similar tasks were performed three times in each experiment.

Measurements of preferences for principles, satisfaction with the principles, and degree of certainty with the ranking of principles were made at each stage of the experiments.[12] In effect the subjects were asked at each stage: "How do you feel now about the principle? How do you rank it now? How sure

12. Satisfaction with the group's choice of principle was measured only after the last production period in the imposed experiments.

Table 5. Marginal Pay Rates

Number of Errors Found and Corrected	Pay for Each Subsequent Error Corrected	Actual Earnings	Yearly Salary
0-4	$0.25		
1		$0.25	$2,080
2		0.50	4,160
3		0.75	6,240
4		1.00	8,320
5-9	1.50		
5		2.50	20,800
6		4.00	33,280
7		5.50	45,760
8		7.00	58,240
9		10.00	83,200
10+	3.00		
10		13.00	108,160
11		16.00	133,120
12		19.00	158,080
13		22.00	183,040
14		25.00	208,000
15		28.00	232,960

are you? How satisfied are you?" Repeating the task and poll allowed us to examine the relationship between attitudes toward the principles and productivity, and to assess changes in attitudes as a function of experience with redistribution.

Performing these tasks and calculating pre- and posttax incomes extended the time required for the experiments. Without abbreviating the original design, the time would have been unacceptably extended. So the first part of the baseline experiment dealing with individual choices of principles and individual payoffs associated with them (see footnote 3) was omitted.

To obtain information on the effect of different levels of democratic participation on attitudes and productivity, the three different treatments in the production experiments used different group-decision rules. In one variant, the choice of principle and tax policy was by unanimous decision; in a second, by majority rule. In the third variation, the group chose neither the principle nor the tax policy. In this case, there was also no group discussion. Instead, the principle that governed the redistribution of their income was imposed by the experimenters. The experiments involving lack of participation could be contrasted with those involving group choices to test for the impact of participation on the acceptability of the principle and its effect on productivity. To control the situation properly, the principle imposed by the experimenters was the one most often chosen by the previous experimental groups.

In all the treatments individuals were familiarized with principles for redistributing income under conditions of impartial reasoning essentially identical to those in the basic experiments. The only difference was that they were told that their future income would depend on how well they did in an unspecified task. Because they did not know whether the task was physical, mathematical, verbal, analytic, or something else, they were not in a position to estimate their future earning potential. Thus they were effectively unable to estimate their likely future productivity and economic status in the production economy.

An outline of the structure of the production experiments and the points at which each of the relevant variables was measured follows.

1. Oral recruitment of five subjects (and when possible two backups) in large university classes.
2. Orientation to the problem of choosing a principle of distributive justice.
3. Measurement of ranking of principles and degree of conviction regarding those rankings.
4. Reading about implications of the principles. Test (and retest when needed) regarding the nature and implications of the principles.

5. Measurement of rankings of principles and degree of conviction.
6. Group discussion and choice (unanimous or majority rule), or imposition of principle.
7. Measurement as in step 3 with measure of satisfaction with principle.
8. First production period and income reported.
9. Measurement as in step 7, but now including consideration of pre- and postredistributive incomes.
10. Second production period and income reported.
11. Measurement as in step 9.
12. Third production period and income reported.
13. Measurement as in step 9.
14. Questionnaire.

PART II

Choices under Conditions of Impartial Reasoning

At certain points, . . . ethical problems do indeed involve "irreducibly personal" choices and considerations; and any proposal to treat the whole of ethics as a single compact discipline would be vain, on that account alone. But this is not—and never could be—the whole story. On the contrary: alongside these personal problems, there are other equally legitimate ethical "points of view," within which the issues raised are unquestionably communal or collective, . . . having to do with . . . the protection of the sick or the poor.

Toulmin (1972, p. 406)

What's best for society, we'd better figure, is best for us. *Transcripts* (p. 328)

CHAPTER FOUR

Basic Results
Impartial Choices

We have argued that impartial reasoning is required to choose an ethically compelling rule for income redistribution and that the incentives in the cake-cutting device can be captured in the laboratory. Individuals can be asked to decide on a redistributive principle without knowing which share they will receive. Persons can be presumed to reason impartially because they do not know their particular interests—which lot may fall to them. The experiments in this book reveal the choices of subjects under these conditions. Because of the incentives to reason impartially, their choices may be deemed "fair" and offer the possibility of revealing a consensus of ethical import on what constitutes distributive justice.

Yet any set of experiments cannot be general; they must rely on specific formulations and employ particular subjects. To preclude too narrow a data base, experiments of several designs were run in three countries at four locations.[1] Students at the University of Manitoba, the University of Maryland, Florida State University, and Warsaw University participated as subjects.[2]

1. Details of the various experimental types are given in Chapter 3. Here we are most immediately concerned with group choices across all types of experiments.

2. We are indebted to our Polish colleagues, who have allowed us to use the

Altogether, ninety-eight experiments provide an empirical basis for testing a variety of hypotheses. The broad contours of the choices made are sketched in this chapter, and the other three chapters in this part are devoted to an analysis of those choices.

Let us recall some of our central questions from Chapter 2:

1. Can individuals reach unanimous agreement on a principle of distributive justice under conditions of impartiality?
2. Will different groups under the same conditions always choose the same principle?
3. Will they choose the "difference principle," as posited by Rawls, to maximize the average utility, as argued by Harsanyi, or some other principle?

Given our methodological argument, we look for the answers to these questions that emerge from the experiments run in the laboratory.

WAS UNANIMITY ACHIEVABLE?

The short answer to whether unanimity was achieved is yes. Subjects almost always reached consensus on a single principle of distributive justice as the "most fair." In the eighty-three experiments in which unanimity was required for agreement,[3] only seven groups (8.4 percent) failed to reach agreement.[4]

The groups that failed to reach unanimous decisions were all

---

results from their experiments as a comparative base. In particular, we thank Wlodzimierz Okrasa, who conceived the notion of replicating our basic experiments in Poland, and G. Lissowski and Tadeus Tyszka, who were instrumental in carrying out the project. We would also like to thank Professor Michael Jackson for help in running two pilot experiments at the University of Sydney. The results were in general agreement with those of the other experiments, but, because of the small numbers, the data from those experiments are not included in this work.

3. In all, ninety-eight experiments were run. In ten the rule was imposed by the experimenters, and in five only a majority of votes was required for agreement.

4. The two groups at the University of Sydney in Australia were also able to achieve unanimity, but their data are not included in the figures. They both chose a principle involving a floor constraint.

in Poland, and there the experiments were inadvertently run under different conditions. Subjects were asked to end their discussion and vote after five minutes rather than to choose when to stop discussion. Under those conditions, seven groups were unable to agree unanimously on a principle. By contrast, in North America, discussion could not be shorter than five minutes and deliberations often went on far longer. Furthermore, when an impasse occurred at North American locations, discussion was to continue if any single person so desired until either a group decision was achieved or all subjects agreed that unanimity was no longer worth pursuing. This provision was included in the instructions for subjects:

> You begin by having a group discussion about which principle you should adopt. The group can terminate this discussion anytime after 5 minutes. If after 5 minutes you feel nothing more can be gained by further discussion, you are to tell this to the moderator. Participants must agree *unanimously by secret ballot* that further discussion is unnecessary for discussion to be ended. . . . Any member of the group can ask for extra discussion, which can be terminated at any time using the procedure described above.

In Poland, however, the experiment was terminated, and the subjects were paid after their first impasse. Polish subjects were not given the opportunity to reconsider and reflect at greater length. Thus, the results are stronger than a superficial evaluation of the data might indicate. In the seventy-six cases, involving 380 subjects in four locations in three countries, when unanimity was sought and no time constraints were enforced, unanimity was always achieved.[5]

And what incentive did the experimental groups have to reach a unanimous decision? It is perhaps best to quote from the book of instructions that governed the experiment itself.

---

5. In a few experiments, a majoritarian rather than a consensual decision rule was used. The failure of the seven groups in Poland to reach unanimous agreement on their first vote is testimony to the impact of the discussion phase on subjects' orientations toward the principles. A premature termination of discussion appears to abort a potentially emerging consensus.

In this part of the experiment you, as a group, are to choose one principle of justice for yourselves. This choice will determine the payoff you get in this part of the experiment. . . . Your choice of principle will be used to pick out those distribution schedules which conform to your principle. Thus, for example, if you picked the principle to maximize the average income, you would be saying that the group wants to pick out a distribution with the highest average income. If there is more than one distribution which has this maximum average income, one will be picked out for you as a group. *Each of you will then be randomly assigned an income from that distribution.* That is your payoff for Part II. . . . Your payoffs in this section of the experiment will conform to the principle which you, as a group, adopt. If you, as a group, do not adopt any principle then we will select one of the income distributions at random for you as a group. That choice of income distribution will conform to no particular characteristics.

Surprisingly, then, even with such a small incentive, almost all groups had little difficulty in reaching agreement. The experimental approximations of the conditions of impartial reasoning were thus capable of generating unanimous decisions about distributive justice.

WAS ANY PRINCIPLE FAVORED?

The principle chosen in the experiments is supportive of neither Rawls's nor Harsanyi's conjecture. The experiments demonstrated an almost total lack of support for the difference principle. Specifically, in only one of the eighty-one experiments in which the groups made a choice did the participants decide to maximize the floor.[6] Indeed, it was the least popular principle![7] Harsanyi fared only slightly better. Only ten groups opted for the principle of maximum income.

6. Here we consider only the eighty-one experiments in which there was choice. We exclude those experiments in which the principle was imposed by the experimenter and those time-constrained Polish experiments in which no choice was agreed on.

7. Even this singleton choice of Rawls's principle may be in error. Our doubts regarding this group's choice are further discussed in footnote 14 in Chapter 5.

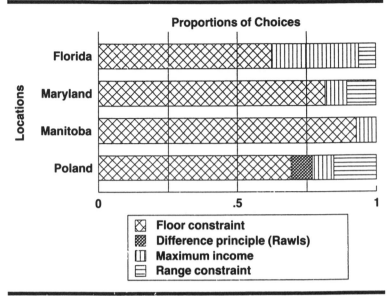

Figure 1. Location of Experiment and Group Choices of Principle

So the two principles argued for were not consistently chosen. But that does not mean that a general consensus was unattainable. A quick glance at Figure 1 shows that considerable agreement was achieved. Groups generally chose a floor constraint.[8] The groups wanted an income floor to be guaranteed to the worst-off individual. This floor was to act as a safety net for all individuals. But after this constraint was set, they wished to preserve incentives so as to maximize production and hence average income. Only occasionally was there a sustained interest in the imposition of a ceiling on incomes (a range constraint).

A floor constraint without a ceiling was dominant across all locations. If we consider the different cultural settings (Manitoba was the home of the only socialist government in North

8. Rawls referred to this as a mixed principle.

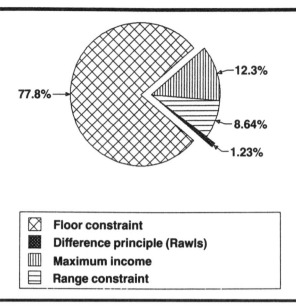

77.8%→

—12.3%

—8.64%

—1.23%

⊠	**Floor constraint**
■	**Difference principle (Rawls)**
ⅢⅢ	**Maximum income**
⊟	**Range constraint**

Figure 2. Distribution of Choices of Principle
(81 Groups)

America at the time; Poland was under a communist regime;
and the United States had Ronald Reagan as president), the
widespread acceptance of the principle is testimony to its cultural robustness. The similarity of the distributions of choices
in the four locations (as displayed in Figure 1) is quite apparent.[9]

The preeminence of floor constraints as a choice is demonstrated graphically in Figure 2, which shows exactly how popular this choice was. In the aggregate, roughly three out of four
groups chose the floor-constraint principle.

9. Recall from our methodological discussion in Part 1 that the experimental method is posited in the notion that there is some diversity in humankind
regarding underlying preferences and attitudes toward aspects of distributive
justice. Thus the experiments are designed to sample and bring these variations, which are so difficult to specify a priori, to bear on the results. A sample
size of five people per experiment might well, therefore, sometimes result in
groups that are somewhat atypical of the sample as a whole. They might well
choose different principles.

ARGUMENTS FOR THE
FLOOR-CONSTRAINT PRINCIPLE

An examination of the conversations subjects had during the course of their deliberations gives us a preliminary sense of why so many groups favored the floor-constraint principle over all others. The discussions were diverse and wide-ranging. Subjects appeared to take the problem they were charged with seriously, and they seemed to be engaged in thoughtful reflection about their decisions. The transcripts of their discussions are far too long to quote at length, but a sampling of their arguments can give the reader a feel for the considerations that came into play.

Most members of virtually all groups were concerned that individuals not fall below a certain minimum level of support. The reasons were concern for both the fate of the individual and the welfare of society:

> I would like to see that everyone at least has the basic things. After that I don't really care. [If the floor is too low] . . . a lot of people are going to be starving, and they will be without shelter and housing. (*Transcripts*, p. 99)

> If you have people that are really really poor, . . . they have a tendency to just stay there because you know there isn't enough nutrition, they can't get an education, and all these kinds of things. But if you put it on a certain minimum, then they have a chance to get out of that situation. They have a chance. (*Transcripts*, p. 72)

> Without a floor . . . you would probably have a lot of crime, which would affect everyone's income in terms of insurance, health costs, etc. (*Transcripts*, p. 2)

Many of the groups also explicitly discussed problems posed by the income redistribution needed to provide an income floor. Some focused on the impact of the floor on recipients of transfers. Most often, they expressed concern that there would be a diminution of the incentive to work if the floor were too high:

But one other thing in here is to maximize the productivity too, and you need to have some kind of incentive there to work hard. (*Transcripts*, p. 116)

SUBJECT I: I think the people need a little bit of incentive to work, and with a floor they just don't get that incentive.

SUBJECT 2:   The average-income person doesn't need help that much. It's the people at the bottom that need help. And they need money help, but they also need incentive help. And that's what we're [up] against. Isn't it? (*Transcripts*, p. 163)

Conversely, the principle of maximum income (no floor, no ceiling) was seen by most groups as being most compatible with individual entitlements and incentives.

SUBJECT I: The best way to bring justice to every individual rather than to a group of individuals would be, in this case, to maximize the average.

SUBJECT 2:   Because that gives the most potential. (*Transcripts*, p. 75)

I'm not worried about most people. If we're talking about a free society, I'm worried what each individual . . . can get out of it with their efforts (*Transcripts*, p. 304)

SUBJECT I: I suggest we choose the thing with the largest range of distributions. That way at least somebody is going to get a real good payoff.

SUBJECT 2:   You're feeling lucky in other words.

SUBJECT I: Listen, in real life the countries that are best off are always those that leave the whole mess alone, that keep government out of the whole thing. No control over averages or floors or anything. (*Transcripts*, p. 313)

A range constraint, however, was seen as being an unnecessary limitation on a natural desire to earn a lot and on a chance to make a killing.

You're going for your selfish motives. You don't want a range constraint because that's going to keep us low. (*Transcripts*, p. 306)

Constraining the range is the least desirable, but I think we definitely need a floor constraint, . . . in terms of justice, [it's] fair. (*Transcripts*, p. 314)

I don't like maximizing the average with a range [constraint] because it restrains people as to how much they can get. I like putting a floor on it because everyone should have a certain subsistence, you know. (*Transcripts*, p. 324)

There was a tension between the desire to preserve entitlements and to ensure that people at the bottom were not too badly off:

I'm actually thinking of the poor people—like, I don't want to see people starve to death, but I don't want anybody to limit my income just because it's some sort of socially adopted policy. (*Transcripts*, p. 194)

SUBJECT 1: People have to pay for this stuff. These floor things don't come for nothing.

SUBJECT 2: Well, it's also a question of justice too. That's quite the issue too. I want to be rich, but I don't want the feeling that there are people hungry.

SUBJECT 1: Justice says that the more you go to school, the more you learn, the more you contribute, the better your income is. That's justice! Welfare is not justice.

SUBJECT 2: Well, I think a civilized society should be able to carry at least 10 percent.

SUBJECT 1: Ten percent! Let's say 2 percent. Let's carry the widows, the orphans, and the crippled. I'd better not say crippled . . . but the people that physically and mentally can't take care of themselves, because the rest of the world can. (*Transcripts*, p. 316)

In most cases groups resolved these conflicting tensions by opting for the mixed principle: a floor without a ceiling. It was viewed as providing a guarantee that no one would "starve" and would also allow those with luck, ambition, or talent (or some combination of these) to increase their earnings without limit and without unnecessary taxation.

Maximize the average with a floor constraint? That's the one that I kind of like too. I like it because you're guaranteed a certain amount of money so you're not going to walk away empty. But then if you have to do harder work or more work, you have a chance to like maximize your profits. (*Transcripts*, p. 138)

In society it seemed if you had a floor constraint there's still no limit as to how much you can make. It might be lowered because there are people who have to make a certain amount, but you could still make a great amount of money in real society. (*Transcripts*, p. 347)

At first I was just thinking: Oh wouldn't it be nice if the people in the lowest—what they call the floor income—if we could maximize that. But then I thought no, because why should I work? I was thinking about myself. Why would I want to work really hard and give them my money? You know. It depends on where you are. In Ocean City nine miles from that condominium there are people living in little shoe boxes, . . . living in poverty. If I was one of those people, yea, I'd want to maximize the floor income. But if I was staying at the Carousel Hotel, I would want to do something else. . . . I decided that, okay, first of all maximizing the average income; to me that gives everybody incentive, but it's like no protection. So then I picked C [floor constraint] because that gives anybody incentive. (*Transcripts*, p. 35)

At some level the discovered patterns in the experiment are highly intuitive. After all, as Hare (1973, pp. 248–249) notes, the setting of a floor, or insurance, is attractive:

Rawls uses arguments in favor of maximining which are really only arguments in favour of insuring against utter calamity. . . . We insure our houses against fire because we think that a certain outcome, namely having one's house burnt down and having no money to buy another, is so calamitous that we should rule it out. This is not at all the same strategy as maximizing [the floor]. If the POL [people-in-ordinary-life] society were going to be affluent enough to provide a more than just acceptable standard of living for even the least advantaged, the insurance strategy would allow the POPs to purchase a very great gain for the more advantaged at the cost of a small loss for the least advantaged; but the maximin strategy would forbid this.

Table 6. Floor Constraints Chosen in the Four Test Locations

	Florida	*Manitoba*	*Maryland*	*Poland*
Number of groups	10	13	29[a]	9
Mean (in dollars)	11,272	10,269	10,983	19,733
Median (in dollars)	10,500	10,500	11,850	21,600
Standard deviation	2,608	2,962	3,901	4,413

[a] Two groups in Maryland chose floor constraints that were not numerical but were a complex function of the mean income. They are not included here.

MAGNITUDE OF THE
FLOOR CONSTRAINTS CHOSEN

Of course, general agreement on a particular principle should not be regarded as absolute agreement across all groups. Despite agreement on a single principle, there were clear differences in the floor constraints set by the different groups. These differences can be analyzed to yield an understanding of the content of the moral positions taken in the laboratory. To the extent that a higher floor places a greater weight on the needs of the worst-off than on the entitlements of the well-off, that decision has a normative content. Factors bearing on this trade-off are analyzed in Chapter 6, but as background it is instructive to examine the distribution of chosen floor constraints.[10]

When the choices are categorized by location, significant variance becomes clear. (See Table 6.) However, it is notable that the mean in North America hovers a bit above the hypothetical poverty level of $10,000 per year. The higher Polish mean and its apparently nonnormal distribution are notable.

10. Recall that the experiments were conducted in three different countries with three different currencies. The differences between Canadian and U.S. dollars may be considered minor, but not those between the Polish zloty and the dollar. Luckily the transformation is not as difficult as one might have thought. Given the scale we were employing, in the middle and late 1980s, $10,000 per year in the United States and Canada was somewhere above or around a threshold of poverty. Similarly, according to our Polish colleagues, during the winter

Factors underlying this and other differences are analyzed in the chapters to come.

---

of 1987–1988, 1,000 zloty per month (based on a twelve-month salary calculation) was near a commonly perceived threshold of poverty in Warsaw. We were able thus to translate the figures easily to something comparable in the North American data. Polish figures can be somewhat directly interpreted as relative to a poverty line of 10,000 units by multiplying by twelve.

CHAPTER FIVE

Explaining Group Choices of Principles

Most groups chose a principle with a floor constraint. This high level of support makes the floor-constraint principle a contender as a fair rule. But near consensus, by itself, is not enough to give floor constraints an ethical status. After all, the choices have ethical validity only to the extent that the experimental conditions engender a degree of impartial reasoning. If the experimental approximations are sufficiently remote from the ideal, we would have to deny ethical significance to any consistent pattern of choices. Thus, limitations in the execution and design of the experiment pose possible threats to the ethical interpretation of the findings. They could undercut the claim that the floor constraint has ethical status. It is therefore necessary to examine the extent to which particular considerations may have impinged on decisions, undermined impartiality, and perhaps determined the group choices.

KNOWING WHO YOU ARE

The experiments diverge from the ideal conditions of impartial reasoning in that the subjects retain a good deal of information. In his development of the conditions of impartial reasoning, Rawls assumes individuals have no significant self-knowledge.

But in reality experimental subjects know who they are. If we could establish that although "some types of people" choose one principle, other "types" choose another, this determination would constitute presumptive evidence that the choices of principle have no claim to universal validity. Any strong relationship between the individuals' characteristics and their choices of principle would cast doubt on the impartiality generated by the experiment.

Only when people cannot calculate the impact of their particular skills, social position, and so forth on their income might their choice of rule have a claim to fairness. Our construct differs from the thought experiments of philosophers in that we believe that the required level of uncertainty can be achieved without removing all particular knowledge from the subjects. In our experiments two different mechanisms were used to restrict the subjects' knowledge of their final economic status: (1) In most of the experiments subjects were randomly assigned an income class after their choice of principle. (2) In a subset of experiments, subjects were told that after a principle had been arrived at they would each be given a task to perform that would generate income based on individual performance. But subjects did not know what the task was. Consequently, they could not know their future earning prospects.

Although these procedures obscure subjects' assignment to income classes, the experiments cannot deny subjects all particular information about themselves.[1] They know their identities, their talents, their tastes, and their social statuses. This knowledge can spill over into the experiments, color the individuals' notions of their self-interest, and bias their decisions. For example, if they feel successful in the real world they may expect to do well in the experimental world. This expectation could affect the degree to which they advocate redistribution. So could other less positive expectations. Socioeconomic char-

---

1. We have argued previously that in any idealized construct it is not useful to remove all particular information from the persons. To do so would be to remove the basis for choice. Nevertheless, it is clear that Rawls means to remove more particular information than we can.

acteristics could impinge on their choices. Indeed, such effects occasionally came through in the discussions. To illustrate, consider the following excerpt:

> We can all say that we're all going to be better off. . . . But is that what we want? Like, I'm planning to be making a hell of a lot of money when I'm over fifty and so on. I wouldn't be expecting to make just an average amount . . . because I don't believe that. (*Transcripts*, p. 287)

But, as noted, we hoped that either their random income assignment or their ignorance about the task facing them would induce substantial uncertainty. Thus, it is gratifying that more often than not this uncertainty was reflected in subjects' comments:

> The reason why I'm suggesting what I'm suggesting is that in this particular instance I would assume that our goal as a group is for each of us to get out of here with as much money as possible. Is that a rational assumption? In order for all of us to get out of here with as much money as possible and since we don't know what the skills are—I mean out in society I am fairly confident that I could get a fairly good amount of money, but the skills out there are the skills that I am aware of that I have and can deliver. We don't know what the skills are here. So I might be able to make the maximum amount; then again my skills may be such that I won't be able to make a penny here under a normal system. So if I can't make any money with my skills, I would like to be able to make some money by ensuring that there is some system that we all get out of here with something more than we came in with. (*Transcripts*, p. 129)

But if we are to ascribe ethical significance to group choices made in a laboratory, we must present more than anecdotal evidence. We must check how the information subjects retain affects both their preferences and their choices of principles. To do so, we analyze subjects' responses to questions about attitudes, social standing, and aspirations, and attempt to relate them to subsequent choices.

In this chapter, we look at these relationships and search for links that could undermine any ethical claim for the result.

Specifically, we hope to establish that these three conjectures are false:

1. The subjects are so homogeneous in their values that the overwhelming popularity of floor constraints simply reflects that homogeneity rather than any universal preference.
2. Variance in the group choices can be explained by the subjects' backgrounds.
3. Group choices are unrelated to individual preferences and values.

Our findings can claim to be generalized only if all these statements are false.

Because we are aware of the restrictiveness of our sample, we must show that it has substantial and relevant variability.[2] We measured the characteristics that we believed most likely to bear on preferences for redistribution. If our subjects showed too little variance in these measures, then they arguably constituted too homogeneous a sample.[3] A significant variability would be helpful in supporting a claim for the generalizability of the findings.

But adequate *variance* is not enough. We must also determine that background factors do not play too large a role. Individual preferences for principles should not be reducible to individual background factors. Only if similar preferences for justice emerge in individuals with divergent backgrounds can we claim that the resultant choice has ethical properties. Only then can the general preference for the floor constraint be presumed to be emergent from a general tendency in humanity and not from a narrow and particular experience. The infrequent choices of other principles might then be interpreted as stemming from disturbing (random or uncontrollable) factors in the experiments.[4]

2. Problems of representativeness are discussed in some detail in Chapter 10.

3. It is difficult to specify what constitutes too little variance. We take the position that if the backgrounds of subgroups of subjects are statistically significantly differentiable, then reasonable variance has been attained; it is not too little.

4. There is always the possibility that some factor, unmeasured in our questionnaire, could account for the variance in group choices. But that is a matter for others to test.

Finally, for a popular choice in the experiments to be evidence for an emergent universal choice about distributive justice, the choices should reflect the preferences of the individuals. Absence of a linkage between individual preferences and the group choices would pose another threat to the ethical claim for the results. If the stated preferences of the individuals cannot explain the group choices, that would indicate that the group choice was prompted by factors other than the judgments and preferences of the subjects. It might indicate that the experimental procedures themselves were so "rigid" or directive (in some sense) that subjects were driven to their choices despite their preferences. Under those circumstances, the floor constraint's broad appeal would again be detached from any presumptive ethical status.

Figure 3 is a flow diagram of the analysis that needs to be performed to test the hypothesis that the group choices properly reflect impartial reasoning. The figure outlines the threats to the validity of the ethical claims of our results. Only if all three tests come out the "right" way can we impute some ethical status to the floor-constraint principle. If something other than the conditions of impartial reasoning (as modeled in our experiments) can explain the group choices, any ethical claims for the choices would be suspect. Let us see what the answers are to the three threatening questions. Unfortunately, to get the needed evidence we must present and analyze a good deal of data.

ARE THE SUBJECTS TOO HOMOGENEOUS? POLES VERSUS NORTH AMERICANS

To investigate diversity, the best comparison is between Poland and North America. That distinction should reveal the greatest cultural and background differences among our subjects. On the face of it, we would expect substantial differences between Polish and North American subjects. If we find no differences, it may be that by sampling university students we have not been able to achieve adequate variance in preferences. However, we might find sizable differences among the subjects. If those

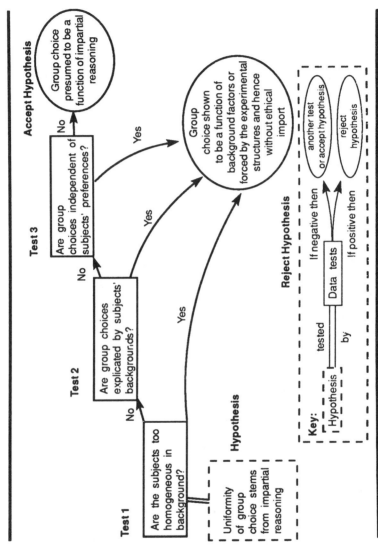

Figure 3. Flow Diagram of Possible Grounds for Rejecting the Ethical Claims of the Results

differences yield little explanatory power over group choices, that would indicate that the similarities in outcome across the experiments do not stem from the subjects' backgrounds. That result would support the conclusion that the results flowed from the impartial reasoning engendered by the design of the experiment.

What are the differences in characteristics and background attitudes of the American and Polish subjects? In our questionnaire, we asked about a variety of socioeconomic attributes, experiences, aspirations, and attitudes. Many significant differences were found among the experimental sites.

Some indicators that varied across sites were quite remote from issues of income redistribution. Some of these differences cause one to wonder whether the differences reflected different sampling patterns as well as different test locations. For example, although the same recruitment methods were used in North America and Poland, the subjects' motives were quite radically different. Three questions were asked to tap the motivation of the subjects for participating in the experiments:[5]

1. My expected monetary reward from this experiment was sufficient to affect my choices.
2. My reason for agreeing to participate in this experiment was to earn money.
3. My reason for agreeing to participate in this experiment was my interest in the project.

Differences in the responses to these questions by Polish and American subjects were highly significant.[6]

Other, socioeconomic and demographic, characteristics varied significantly. Polish students were an average of two years older, and they financed the costs of attending a university quite differently. These differences were also reflected in highly significant divergences in economic aspirations.[7]

5. These questions were answered on a five-point agreement scale. The higher the score, the greater the agreement with the statement.
6. Differences on the first two questions were significant at the .001 level and for the third question at the .02 level.
7. We asked such questions as "What minimum annual income (in thousands of today's dollars [zlotys]) do you think you will find satisfactory as your starting salary for your first job after graduation?"

There was also considerable variation between the Polish and North American subjects on a number of attitudinal variables. They had different views of the role of the individual: "The greatest accomplishments in history were individual efforts." They exhibited different attitudes toward minority groups. Attitudes toward risk also varied. For example, the Polish students were significantly more likely to see lifetime income to be a function of luck, and they described themselves as significantly less oriented toward getting rewards from helping others in life.

In sum, there were underlying differences between the Polish and the North American subjects' backgrounds, motivations, and values. All the differences mentioned were statistically significant at a probability level of at least .05. Although no absolute measure can be adduced to say that these differences were big enough to represent a broad slice of humanity, their statistical variation can assure us that the groups were not superficially homogeneous. We therefore conclude with a negative answer to the first question we posed. The groups are not too homogeneous to threaten our conclusions.

CAN GROUP CHOICES BE EXPLAINED BY SUBJECTS' BACKGROUNDS?

The negative answer to the first question leads us directly to posing the next. Can background characteristics and attitudes predict the choices made in the experiments? Alternatively, do the experimental conditions limit the impact of background factors on group choices and thus support the claim that the subjects engaged in impartial reasoning?

Recall there was considerable agreement among the experimental groups: 78 percent of all groups chose some level of floor. (The reader may wish to reexamine Figure 2.) In asking what difference the backgrounds of the subjects made, we must compare groups that made their decisions under similar experimental conditions.[8] A direct and intuitive test of the effect of

8. In North America there was a variety of experimental conditions. In Po-

Table 7. Principles Chosen in Poland versus
Those Chosen in North America

	Poland	*North America*
Floor constraint	9 groups	14 groups
Range constraint	2	0
Maximum income	1	0

differences in background on group choice can be obtained by comparing choices in North America and Poland under the regular experimental conditions. Even a cursory examination of Table 7 makes it apparent that there is little difference between the Polish and North American distributions of group choices of principle.[9] The floor constraint dominates in both locations. Those differences that do exist are statistically insignificant.[10]

But the fact that the patterns of choices in North America and Poland are similar does not lay to rest our concern that social and attitudinal characteristics might affect group choices. A finer approach is called for. Can the relevant variables be brought to bear in explaining the groups' choices? Ideally we

---

land all experiments were of one type. Thus, in comparing subject pools it is important to look at subjects who made their decisions under comparable conditions. The comparable experiments in North America were those we shall call "regular." Restricting the analysis to only those individuals who were recruited to regular experiments in no way changes the results reported to this point.

9. Only those experiments in North America that were of the same type (that is, regular) are reported in this table. We also do not show the single case in which a Polish group chose the difference principle because in the subsequent analysis we have to exclude that case: a single observed choice would not contain enough variance to be included in the model. Besides, as noted in footnote 14 below, that choice is suspect.

10. This result is confirmed by a statistical test: chi-square = 2.767, df = 2, p = .251. Levels of significance of statistical results are reported as the probability that the results could have occurred as a function of statistical accident. In this case, for example, the odds that this result is an artifact of a statistical accident are about 1:3. Another bit of confirmatory evidence can be found by comparing the distribution of choices across experimental sites. Recall that this pattern showed considerable similarities (reexamine Figure 1).

would like to find out the degree to which background factors determine this choice. The statistical method best suited to this determination is LOGIT.[11] It finds the best model of the independent variables (the background variables) to predict a group's choice of the dependent variable (in this case, a principle).

Recall our concern. Successfully predicting the groups' choices of principles by using individual subjects' characteristics would lead us to doubt that the subjects used impartial reasoning. Thus, results that show no relationship support the argument that the floor-constraint principle has a valid ethical claim.

Fortunately for the hypothesis and the reader, the results of the LOGIT analysis are both easy to report and easy to interpret. The individual background variables play no significant role in explaining the groups' choices of principles. The individual factors that we identified as being different across geographical groups have no explanatory power in identifying choices of principles. Both as a set and individually, they fail to predict choices.

Thus, the answer to our second question is also supportive of the notion that the floor constraint has a claim to ethical status. The subjects from North America and Poland were shown to diverge in many ways, and so the samples drawn appear to represent heterogeneous populations. And yet the experiments appear to have generated homogeneous results. Thus the resultant choices appear not to follow from individual differences. Rather, they may emerge from a sense of justice accessed via the modeled conditions of impartial reasoning.

ARE GROUP CHOICES RELATED TO PREFERENCES?

We still must answer our third question. After all, the following argument would be consistent with our reported results:

11. The choice of principle is a categorical variable. LOGIT is explicitly "designed for the logistic regression analysis of categorical response data . . . [and] is appropriate for analyzing the determinants of a categorical dependent variable" (Steinberg 1985, p. 1). A solid introduction to LOGIT may be found in Aldrich and Nelson (1984).

1. The backgrounds of the individuals are different
2. The background characteristics of the individuals make little difference to group choices
3. The distribution of group choices is relatively uniform across the sites

But

4. The choices do not reflect individual preferences; rather, the choices are generated by the structure of the experiments in some rigid way

Thus:

5. The results do not appear to be the product of individual preferences under impartial reasoning and so fail to shed light on distributive justice.

The threat to our claims posed by item 4 is clear. Under conditions of impartial reasoning, group choice should reflect the considered judgment of subjects. If the preferences of the subjects are not reflected in their choices, our chain of argument is broken. To maintain our contention that the floor-constraint principle has an ethical claim, we must establish that the choices of the groups relate to the attitudes and preferences of the subjects.[12]

The reader oriented toward social choice should feel comfortable with the following discussion. Social-choice theory (and common sense) would lead one to expect a strong relationship between the distribution of preferences at the time of the choice and the outcome of the group choice. Indeed, given the lack of other relations, if this were not the case, we would worry that the results of the experiment, though consistent, were arbitrary.

Let us begin considering the evidence bearing on this question by examining the individual's preferences just before the groups chose. If preferences matter, for example, groups choosing a floor constraint should have had a higher average ranking

---

12. For good measure, if we can establish the link between preferences and choices, we should check to be sure that we cannot explain the preferences of the subject by their backgrounds.

Table 8. Group Choices and Mean Score of Individual Preferences
prior to Discussion

Principle Chosen by Group	Maximum Floor	Maximum Income	Floor Constraint	Range Constraint
Maximum Floor	*10.00*	11.00	26.00	13.00
(N = 5)	(14.14)	(7.42)	(5.48)	(10.95)
Maximum Income	6.63	*22.25*	20.92	10.20
(N = 49)	(9.76)	(9.19)	(7.75)	(9.24)
Floor Constraint	7.93	16.31	*24.71*	11.10
(N = 275)	(9.23)	(10.26)	(7.27)	(9.74)
Range Constraint	11.48	15.00	20.19	*13.33*
(N = 27)	(8.64)	(12.63)	(9.95)	(11.52)
F	1.68	5.56	5.90	.657
p	.17	.001	.001	.579

Standard deviations are in parentheses. The numbers are reduced
due to missing data on some subjects

of the floor-constraint principle than those who chose another
principle. The data are straightforward. (See Table 8.) For the
two most popular principles, setting a floor constraint and
maximum income, the social-choice model appears to be
solid.[13] Looking at the table, we see that the single most dramatic datum is the comparison of the support for maximum
income when that principle was chosen as opposed to when it
was not. Only when those who preferred maximum income
chose it did any principle (other than the floor constraint) score
above 20. Only groups choosing maximum income gave higher
support to it than to the floor constraint.

13. The scores represent the position of the four main principles in the preference rankings of the individuals: first place gets 30, second place gets 20,
third place gets 10, and last place gets 0.

Given the means of the scores, we expect that the preferences for the maximum-income and floor-constraint principles will play a role in explaining group choices. They should show up as highly significant in explaining the outcomes of the group choice.[14] We can directly test for the relationship between preferences (just prior to the group choice) and group choices. A LOGIT model should be able to predict group choices on the basis of individual preferences. And it does.[15] Preferences for the floor-constraint principle and maximum income yield a LOGIT model with a chi-square value of 22.28, significant at the .001 level. The import of this finding can be described simply. There is a strong relationship between individuals' preferences for principles and choice. So it appears that the social choices of the groups follow the preferences of the individuals.

Another test of this critical relationship is the relationship between indirect measures of preferences and the group choices. Attitudes toward different aspects of redistribution are possible indicators of underlying preferences for principles. Because the four principles under consideration involve different degrees and types of redistribution, these attitudes should provide some explanatory power in predicting group choices. An index of support for income redistribution was constructed by adding the scores of the subjects' responses to the following four statements:[16]

1. Relative equality of wealth is a good thing.
2. Government ought to have programs which give money to people like me when unavoidable events interrupt our ability to support ourselves.

14. The alert reader may notice that the one group that chose to maximize the floor did so even though it ranked the principle it chose lowest and the floor constraint highest! It is possible that this case reflects a recording (or other) error that we were unable to identify further. The experiment was conducted in Poland.

15. We restrict the observations to those cases when the three most popular principles were chosen, because only one group chose to maximize the floor.

16. Scoring of these variables is discussed in footnote 5. There is also significant variation between Polish and North American subjects on these questions.

3. A proper role of government is to modify the distribution of earned income.
4. Governments should ensure that all poor people can afford a relatively decent standard of living.

Because these measures reflect differing degrees of support for separable aspects of income redistribution, we should be able to explain some proportion of the groups' choices of principles using this index.[17] And again we can, albeit at a marginal rate. The index is a significant predictor of the group's choice of principle. This result is again supportive of the hypothesized relationship. Preferences regarding income distribution in general are significant predictors of group choices of principles.[18]

Taken together, then, the two LOGIT models indicate a significant relationship between preferences and choices. The strong dominance of the floor-constraint principle cannot be attributed to a structural rigidity in the experimental procedures.

CONCLUSIONS

Looking primarily at the contrast between Poland and North America, we identified a number of significant differences in the background characteristics of the subjects. The differences were sufficiently great for us to conclude tentatively that our sample is not narrowly selected and homogeneous. These variables did not yield any powerful explanatory power with regard to the group choices of principles when they were used as the basis of a statistical model. Yet we did find that the groups'

17. In light of our previous concern about possible homogeneity of subjects, it is worth nothing that subjects in Poland and North America were characteristically different in their responses to these questions. And in the case of three of the four variables, these differences were statistically highly significant (at better than the .001 level). The one statement where the differences were not significant was "Relative equality of wealth is a good thing."

18. The overall model has a chi-square of 6.42, with 2 degrees of freedom. This result is quite a bit less significant than that for the previous model, which used direct preferences for principles as predictors, but still the probability that it fails to explain group choices is less than .05.

choices reflected the attitudes of the members about the principles.

What then are the lessons? There is little evidence that exogenous variables (those outside the experimental design), such as attitudes and backgrounds of subjects, had any significant effect on which principles the groups chose. Under our representation of the conditions of impartial reasoning, the experimental result seems to be robust. In the aggregate, in the context of a group discussion and decision, individual differences appear to be harmonized to yield a consensual decision. The group choice in such cases can, in general, be predicted to be a floor income that does not otherwise constrain incentives to maximize income.

These findings furnish strong presumptive evidence for the impact of the experimental treatment in inducing the group choice. They support the notion that the sample of subjects is diverse but that this approximation of the conditions of impartial reasoning can filter antecedent differences and yield a principle that has a claim to ethical validity. Deviations from this pattern seem to reflect (weakly) such random elements as the path of discussions and the initial predispositions toward other distributive principles.[19] But the effects of such deviations are neither strong nor frequent. Relatively large differences in these initial conditions often had little or no effect on the outcome. Or, using the words of James Gleick, there appears to be no "butterfly effect."[20]

Although these differences in background variables and individual preferences cannot explain choices of principles, there is another choice to be explained. The groups chose different floor levels. Perhaps these differences are explicable? We turn to that question in the next chapter.

19. These factors will be analyzed further in Chapter 7.
20. "Tiny differences in input could quickly become overwhelming differences in output—a phenomenon given the name 'sensitive dependence on initial conditions.' In weather, for example, this translates in to what is only half-jokingly known as the Butterfly Effect—the notion that a butterfly stirring the air today in Peking can transform storm systems next month in New York" (Gleick 1987, p. 8).

CHAPTER SIX

Group Choices
of a Floor Constraint

As we have seen, group choices of a principle appear to be robustly independent of differences in the values of the individuals in the group. The choices seem to emerge from the discussion and the exercise of impartial reasoning as induced by the experimental conditions. In most cases the groups chose not only a principle but also a floor constraint to cushion the fate of the worst-off. Those support levels varied.

We can attempt to explain the dollar value of the floor just as we attempted to explain the groups' choices of principles. We can ask: Why do experimental groups that agree to the same principle (a floor constraint) set the constraints at such different levels? Perhaps these differences can be explained by the underlying values and attitudes in the groups. That analysis requires a statistical approach, but, as a prelude, a sampling of the discussions can convey the flavor of the arguments used by the subjects.

Three factors entered into many of the deliberations. Subjects voiced concerns about entitlements, incentives, and the need to ensure a Spartan existence for the poor. The conflict among these factors is evident in their dialogue:

SUBJECT 1: Now if we have a floor constraint of $18,000, people are going to say, "Huh, forget it; I'm not going to get a degree!"

SUBJECT 2: Forget it. I'm not going to work. (*Transcripts*, p. 221)

SUBJECT 1:   There needs to be a floor constraint. You can have it high; you can have it low. But they should have some type of constraint where . . . they would be able to be taken care of.

SUBJECT 2:   Yeah, but if you set your floor constraint below subsistence?

SUBJECT 3:   Well, that's where incentive comes in.

SUBJECT 1:   That's where incentive comes in. I mean they're not dirt poor. I mean at least they have some stake, some start. (*Transcripts*, p. 41)

If you pick a floor constraint too high, then it's kind of like doing number 1, . . . kind of like maximizing the floor. (*Transcripts*, p. 321)

SUBJECT 1:   If the floor is say $10,000, you know that that is enough to sustain you at a basic level of existence— shelter, food. You're not going to be eating caviar on that either.

SUBJECT 2:   It's to encourage you to get more money.

SUBJECT 1:   Right! You'll make more money if you work harder. We won't let you starve to death, but if you want any more you're going to have to work for it. (*Transcripts*, p. 84)

A number of the groups drew careful distinctions between the "deserving" and "undeserving" poor and were concerned that a floor would protect the undeserving at the expense of taxpayers:

Well, we have a problem deciding whether it'll be with a floor because they don't work or if there's a floor because they're just poor. (*Transcripts*, p. 63)

In the end, the floor constraints chosen exhibited a roughly normal distribution in North America and were somewhat higher in Poland. They reflected these concerns but exhibited considerable variance.

To explain that variance we again report many of the group's properties as statistical aggregates of those of their constituent members. The choices are group choices, and so we use the average value of the group member's background characteristics to explain the variations in the level of floor constraints chosen.

We analyze sixty-one floor constraints.[1] More than one-half of the observations lie between $10,000 and $14,000 (see Table 9). Yet one observation is as low as $2,000, while others are at $24,000. But recall that we had many different experimental treatments. Specific cues in each of the experimental conditions may have affected the behavior of the subjects in the experiments. This possibility leads to a hypothesis: The type of experiment (such as a focus on ethical rather than self-interested aspects or on gains rather than losses) explains much of the variance in the level of the floor chosen in the experiment.

Another possible explanation for the different levels of floors chosen is that the floor is the outcome of a five-person bargaining situation. If the individuals bargain over the substantive level of a floor support and each individual has a different notion of the appropriate level, the outcome might be a compromise. We can ask whether some background variables are good predictors of subjects' preferences for different levels of constraints. This question prompts a second hypothesis: The level of the constraint chosen by a group can be predicted from the means of variables that measure the background and values of the individuals in each group. We look at each of these hypotheses in turn and then together.

TYPE OF EXPERIMENT AS DETERMINANT OF THE FLOOR

Did our manipulation of the experimental conditions (setting up slightly different representations of the conditions of impartial reasoning) have an effect on the level of floor that was set? To address this question, we use the reduced data set of 52

---

1. Sixty-three groups set a floor constraint. In two of these cases the constraint was a function of the average income and other factors and did not have a numerical value.

Table 9. Distribution of Floor Constraints

Number of groups	61	Maximum	24,000
Minimum	2,000	Upper quartile	13,000
Lower quartile	10,000	Mean	12,169
Median	12,000	Standard deviation	4,759

Size of Constraint (thousands of dollars)	Each Digit Represents an Observation[a]
2	0
3	6
4	
5	0
6	001
7	5
8	0005
9	0
10	0000000000055
11	00058
12	000000000558
13	0000
14	0045
15	07
16	
17	2
18	00
19	
20	
21	66
22	
23	4
24	000

[a] Each digit is the number of hundreds of dollars of the choice above the thousands of dollars indicated in the left column. Thus, the 6 in the second row is a floor set at $3,600.

experiments completed in North America in which the floor-constraint principle was chosen.[2]

This question should be answered for pairs of competing experimental conditions. Specifically, experiments differed with regard to: (1) whether justice was ever mentioned as a normative concern, (2) the degree of variability of the payoffs in the early stages of the experiments (high or low), and (3) in the final stage whether the payoff was a loss from a credit already granted the subject (rather than a gain). We can treat each of these test conditions as binary distinctions and examine whether any pair of treatments made a significant difference in the level of constraint chosen.

One simple method of testing for the effect of these conditions on the levels of constraints is to see whether the differences in the mean constraints chosen across treatments are significant. The results of these t-tests are shown in Table 10. None of the differences are significant at the .05 level. The type of experimental treatment appears to have made no significant difference in the level of the floor constraint chosen by the groups.[3] Thus, the status of our first hypothesis is clear: the experimental conditions do not explain the level of constraint chosen by the groups.

INDIVIDUAL CHARACTERISTICS
AS DETERMINANTS OF THE FLOOR

In Chapter 5 we identified a number of socioeconomic variables that correlated significantly with preferences for principles and that appeared to be quite variable across Poland and North America. They were used in an attempt to relate group choices of principles to individual preferences for principles. Although those results were relatively unsuccessful, we can

2. Because only one type of experiment was conducted in Poland and because the experiments in Poland often yielded a floor very different from that set in North America, we do not apply the Polish data to this question.

3. Even with all the Polish cases considered, none of the tests is significant at the .05 level. Indeed, we can ask whether using an alternative approach—a regression analysis with the three treatment variables taken as binary categori-

Table 10. Mean Choice of Level of Floor Constraints by Experimental Type

Test for:	Mean	Mean	t^a	p
Justice versus nonjustice (Maryland)	12,125	12,413	0.37	.723
Number of groups	4	4		
Gain versus loss (Manitoba)	10,357	10,167	0.11	.914
Number of groups	7	6		
Gain versus high gain (Maryland)	12,125	9,770	1.50	.171
Number of groups	4	6		
Loss versus high loss (Florida)	10,667	10,000	0.48	.653
Number of groups	3	4		
High gain versus high loss (Florida and Maryland)	9,770	10,000	0.14	.889
Number of groups	6	4		

[a] These significance tests are done with very small $\underline{N}$s to ensure that we are holding everything except the conditions as constant as possible. Because there was not a complete crossing in the experimental design (that is, we did not run all types in all locations), larger $\underline{N}$s would require that we compare one type of experiment (for example, gain) done in one or more locations with another type (for example, nonjustice) done in other locations. Such significance tests were also run; the results remained statistically insignificant.

again try to use these variables to ask how well they explain the level of the constraints chosen by the groups. After all, it is possible that the choice of principle is emergent from the experimental conditions because it reflects the fruits of impartial reasoning, while the level of the constraint reflects the results of a slightly different process: bargaining among subjects who are bringing to bear their particular values, which are not masked by the laboratory conditions. Were this the case, background characteristics and underlying values, such as attitudes toward income distribution, could prove important in explaining the level of the constraint chosen.

To assess this possibility, we use the same stepwise regression procedures employed previously.[4] That procedure allows us to identify which of the background variables appear to have power in explaining differences in groups' choices of floor-constraint levels. The startling result of this analysis is that none of the demographic or socioeconomic variables survive the standard test of statistical significance. Only one variable shows any significant explanatory power and it is the same attitudinal variable that allowed for a modest prediction of group choice: the index of attitudes toward income redistribution. This time the explanation it provides is quite good. For the sample as a whole, the nature of the linear relationship is depicted in Figure 4. Pearson's R is .67, and 44 percent of the variance in the level of the floor constraint is explained by subjects' attitudes toward income redistribution. In other words, there is a strong and positive link between support for income redistribution in general and the acceptable level of a floor income.[5]

Given the strength of this relationship, it is of interest to see whether it bears up when North America and Poland are

---

cal variables—will yield some explanatory power. Again, the answer is no. No treatment variable is significant, and virtually none of the variance is explained.

4. Because we use ideology and other measures of socioeconomic status that were not recorded in Poland, we reduce the sample to North America. A similar analysis of the Polish data led to the same conclusions.

5. One variable that, ex ante, might have been expected to have powerful

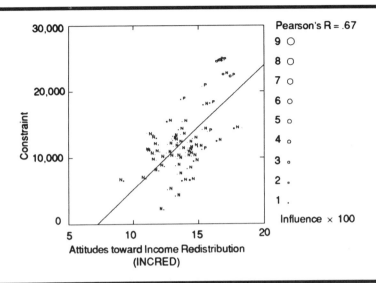

Figure 4. Relationship of the Level of Constraint Chosen to Attitudes toward Income Redistribution

Note: N stands for a North American data point; P, for Polish. The size of any circle reflects the degree of influence of that single observation on the regression line. Large circles show that single data points have substantial influence on the regression results. Influences that increase the correlation are shown by a hollow circle. Solid circles are those that decrease the correlation. The equation for the regression line is: floor constraint = 13,645 + 1,885(INCRED). The adjusted R^2 is .434. It is highly significant (F = 47.0, P < .0005). N = 61.

treated separately. Figures 5 and 6 show the scatter plots of those two subsets of data. Do we get comparable results from the two data sets? The simple answer is yes. There are similarities between the linear fits in the two cases. In both we find that the data support a clear, positive relationship. Higher sup-

---

explanatory power was a notable failure. Ideology as self-reported on a liberal-to-conservative five-point scale explained none (0.000) of the variance in the level of the floor chosen by the groups. It was insignificant.

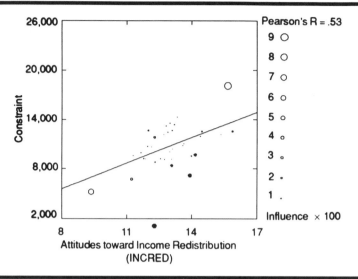

Figure 5. Relationship of the Level of Constraint Chosen to Attitudes toward Income Redistribution: North America

Note: Each observation is a single group choice of a floor-constraint principle. $\underline{N}$ = 52. For an explanation of this figure, see Figure 4.

port for the notion of income redistribution is positively related to choices of higher floors.[6] We obtained a Pearson's R of .53 and .56 for North America and Poland, respectively. However, the impact of support for income redistribution appears to be higher in Poland than in North America. In Poland increased support for income redistribution leads to higher levels of floor support (the best-fit line is steeper in the Polish graph).

LOCATION AS DETERMINANT OF THE FLOOR

We can text explicitly for how much location helps to explain the level of the floor chosen by inserting it into the regression equation. The result is dramatic! Including a categorical loca-

6. Of course, in Poland the plot is only suggestive; there are too few data points to develop regression coefficients and other statistics with confidence.

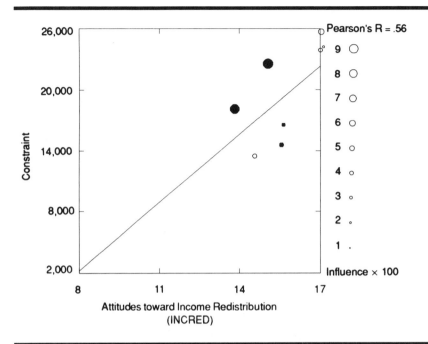

Figure 6. Relationship of the Level of Constraint Chosen to Attitudes toward Income Redistribution: Poland

Note: Each observation is a single group choice of a floor-constraint principle. $\underline{N}$ = 8. One outlying constraint that was an order of magnitude larger was dropped because of undue influence. For an explanation of this figure, see Figure 4.

tion variable yields a Pearson's *R* of .76, indicating that 57 percent of the variance in levels of the floor constraint can be explained. Two variables—location and the index of support for income redistribution—explain over half the variance in the floor levels chosen.

CONCLUSIONS

We are able to explain much in the group setting of a floor. There is a strong positive link between the average support for income redistribution by members of the group and the level of the floor constraint they agree on. Polish subjects support higher floors than do their North American counterparts. By contrast, there are solid indications that relationships to other variables, such as ideology, risk aversion, or satisfactory-salary projections, are weak. Other sociopolitical variables appear to have relatively little power in explaining the level of the floor.

We have argued that an experiment designed to induce impartial reasoning should nullify individual background characteristics as factors that explain choices. The choices should flow from arguments based on an impartial point of view. In Chapter 5 that desired effect was obtained. The choice of principle was shown to be effectively independent of subjects' individual characteristics. Here, we have shown that one element of the decision—the level of the floor—can be explained. Does this result mean that our attempt to negate individual factors has failed, and that the results of the experiments do not represent general propensities in humanity? We do not think so. We believe that the ability to predict the level of the floor does not undercut the ethical validity of the result.

In contrast to the emergent and almost universal consensus on one principle, the setting of the floor can be thought of as an outcome to a bargaining problem among the individuals (much as Harsanyi and Rawls wanted it). A substantial proportion of the discussion time was devoted to arguments about the appropriate level of the floor constraint. It was a negotiable, quantifiable component of the bargaining. Each group's decision was a result of pulling and hauling on the part of individuals with different preferences. Moreover, the level of the floor represents a tradeoff between two competing ethical values and one positive incentive. The values are recognition of the need of those who cannot earn enough income to reach the floor and recognition of the entitlements of those who work and earn. The incentive in question is the need to encourage both those below the floor to become productive and those above it to continue producing. A high floor gives more weight to need and less to entitlements, and can potentially reduce incentives. A low floor does the opposite. Thus individuals who place different weight on the competing values and have different views of the role of incentives will have preferences for different floor levels.

Rawls and Harsanyi anticipated such bargaining but were unable or unwilling to identify the nature of the tradeoffs that would take place among individuals doing the bargaining. Indeed, it was virtually impossible for them to specify which components of preference would be allowed to remain in the psyches of the individual bargainers to generate a deterministic result. We would argue that this difficulty—the problem of anticipating the outcome of a bargain among "representative" but underspecified individuals—is a further argument for the use of experimental methods. A significant diversity of individual perspectives must be captured in the bargaining. Introspection and projection furnish too thin a tool on too narrow a base to allow a single theorist to anticipate what a representative sample of humanity might decide under conditions of impartiality.[7] Real representatives may be required.

Moreover, any individuals faced with the task of setting a floor income need some context. Rawls describes the setting as one of moderate scarcity. That covers quite a range. The United States and China might both be characterized that way, but citizens of the two countries might well and reasonably disagree on what constitutes a "fair" floor income. That judgment is made relative to their context and their experience. The Chinese "fair" floor would certainly be set below the American. But the principle invoking the need for a floor might well be invariant.

The necessity of infusing experience and context into at least one aspect of the decision points out the difficulty of relying solely on abstract theoretical arguments such as the veil

7. It is difficult to imagine how any degree of prior thought on the part of a theorist could have projected the results that were achieved. Who, for example, could have expected that differences in political ideology are not significantly related to chosen levels of a floor constraint under conditions approximating those of impartial reasoning?

of ignorance to determine the outcome. It may be necessary to model the conditions and let subjects provide the content or parameters that are hard to specify *ex ante*. The outcomes then emerge from the laboratory approximation as a result of a robust interaction among subjects. That some aspects of the outcomes cannot be explained fully while others can is testimony to the difficulty of specifying a priori what information individuals should be allowed to retain and bring to bear on their decisions. It underlines the need for, and potential efficacy of, an empirical approach that teases out the content of impartial reasoning.

CHAPTER SEVEN

The Role of Experimental
Factors in Individual Choices

We have seen that experimental groups in four locations are able to reach consensus on a principle. Their overwhelming preference is for a principle that sets an income floor. Furthermore, the choices reflect individual preferences, not aggregate background characteristics. We would therefore like to conclude that the choice of a floor constraint has ethical validity.

But such a conclusion is still premature. It is possible that the consensus reported simply reflects subjects' antecedent notions of what is just. We might simply be reporting the results of their initial preferences. Were that true, the experiments would be no more than a survey of preferences and would not be a meaningful evocation of impartial reasoning. To check for this possibility we now probe into the bases of all those unanimous decisions. Do the individuals all develop the same preference structures during the experiments, or, alternatively, do they walk in with the same preferences and maintain them? Does the unanimity represent their individual preferences or is it a compromise position?

If the groups' choices are to have ethical validity, the answer to the following central question must be positive: Does the structure of the experiments affect the subjects' preferences and choices? We are concerned that the experiments make a

95

difference. Participating in the experiments must have a meaningful impact on the subjects if the experiments are to reveal anything about distributive justice. After all, if the experiments are not changing opinions, we are simply reporting antecedent dispositions. And no theory of justice should be based on a simple reporting of attitudes. We must therefore be sure that we have gone beyond a reporting of prior rigid beliefs if we are to generalize what happens in the particular groups we examine. Then, and only then, can we show that the experimental results provide valid insight into the nature of distributive justice.

In Chapter 5 we explored the relationship between group choice and individual preferences and demonstrated that preferences mattered. Now we must explore another aspect of these relationships. Specifically, do individuals' preferences change over the course of the experiments? And if they do, how? Do subjects gain or lose confidence in their preferences? Do different experimental groups behave differently? Answers to these questions address both the substantive issue of the attractiveness of various principles and the methodological issues of the internal and external validity of the experiments.

What can we say about the consensus that emerged in groups? If we look at the seventy-six experimental groups in which unanimity was both required and achieved, we find some surprises. In only twenty (26 percent) of these experiments did all the individuals' preferences agree with the unanimous group choice. In 74 percent of the cases some individuals had a preferred principle that differed from the one chosen by the group. It is relevant to these results that Rawls indicated that a unanimous group decision need not reflect complete agreement among individuals regarding a principle.[1] Rather, it was to reflect a workable political consensus. Our results support that interpretation: the decision is usually the result of political compromise, at least by some of the individuals.

1. This was his position during extended private conversations at a conference in Halifax in the summer of 1984. These comments about the nature of unanimity were not made in a public forum.

CHANGES IN INDIVIDUAL PREFERENCES

If the experiments make a difference in individuals' preferences, there should be measurable shifts both in subjects' rankings of principles and in their confidence in those rankings. To see whether changes do occur we can first look at the relationship between subjects' initial preferences and the group's choice. Indeed, in only five of seventy-six groups reaching consensus did the individuals agree, at the time of the first measure, on their first choice of principles. In four of these groups, this consensus on first rankings was repeated after the group choice is made. But in only one of the groups did the agreement hold up over the entire course of the experiment. In other words, even when a group walked into the experiment with initial unanimity regarding the best choice, their experiences over the course of the experiment led them (individually) to waver in their support.

But much more data can be brought to bear on this question. Recall that preference rankings were measured at the beginning of the experiments, after the test, prior to the decision phase, and after the decision (see Chapter 3).[2] The subjects' experience can be broken into two distinct phases: all activities prior to the group discussion; and the group discussions and decision.[3] We can examine the data to see whether these two experiences made a difference.

Changes Prior to Discussion and Decision

Let us begin by looking at individuals' initial preferences. What was their most-preferred principle when they were first asked? These responses constitute a baseline for gauging change. (See

2. In the production experiments they were also taken after each production stage. We will discuss the impact of production on preferences later. Here we focus on the first, third, and fourth measurement of preferences to identify the impact of various phases of the experiments on subjects.

3. In one variant of the production experiments the principle was imposed by the experimenters. In this discussion we leave those data in for the prediscussion analysis. We take them out in our separate analysis and contrast of the effect of the discussion and imposition treatments on individual preferences.

the first row of data in Table 11.)[4] Clearly the floor constraint is the runaway most popular principle. It receives first-place rankings from 57 percent of the subjects. Maximum income is a distant second, and, perhaps surprisingly, Rawls's principle—maximizing the floor income—is dead last. It receives only 10 percent of the subjects' first rankings.

The second row presents the first-place rankings of principles after the first part of the experiment and just prior to the decision phase. The third row presents the difference between the first two rows: the net changes in first-place rankings over that period. On a net-change basis there would appear to be considerable stability. The most popular principle gains only one first-place ranking over this period. The principle of maximum income is the biggest winner: it gains a net of twenty-three first-place rankings at the expense of the other principles. Twenty-four net changes in 414 individuals would seem to indicate stability of preferences. But one ought not to use net stability as a precise measure of changes in preferences.

To see whether the experiment was affecting preferences we need a way of showing all shifts in first-place rankings: not just the net changes. These gross changes are shown in rows 4 and 5 of the table. Those rows show all gains and losses of first-place rankings from the outset to just prior to the decision. Any switch in first-place preferences shows up both as a gain for one principle (in row 4) and as a loss for another (in row 5). The apparent stability represented by the small net changes in row 3 hides another reality: 119, or 29 percent, of the subjects changed their choice of most-preferred principle. Furthermore, there are great differences in the stability of the subjects' preferences as a function of which of the principles is ranked first. So maximizing the floor had eighteen losses out of forty supporters (for a 45 percent desertion rate); maximum income had

---

4. In Tables 11–14, for simplicity, missing data and tied rankings are omitted. Thus, when sequential measures are compared, only those without missing data and having no ties are used unless otherwise indicated. But the basic patterns remain regardless of how we handle missing data.

Table 11. Shifts in Individuals' First-Place Rankings of Principles prior to Discussion

	Maximum Floor	Maximum Income	Floor Constraint	Range Constraint	Total
1. Start of experiment	40	83	237	54	414
2. Prior to discussion	30	106	238	40	414
3. Net changes	*-10*	*23*	*1*	*-14*	0
4. Gross gains	8	51	45	15	119
5. Gross losses	-18	-28	-44	29	-119
6. Desertion rate (line 5/line 1)	.45	.34	.19	.54	.29

Note: These individuals were all in choice experiments and had non missing data at both measures.

twenty-eight deserters out of eighty-three (a 34 percent rate); the range constraint had twenty-nine deserters out of fifty-four (54 percent); but the floor constraint had only a 19 percent defection rate (44 out of 237). (See Figure 8 later in this chapter.) Overall, however, the matrix of preference switches reveals that the net changes are the result of considerable shifting of preferences over the course of the first phase of the experiments.

Any shifts in preference can connote either growing uncertainty or a consolidation because of learning and reflection. Only if consolidation takes place can the experimental conditions be argued to be promoting a reflective equilibrium among subjects. To monitor uncertainty/consolidation, subjects were asked: "How do you feel about your ranking of these principles?" each time they ranked the principles. The responses were recorded on a five-point Likert scale from very unsure (1) to very sure (5). Their responses at the different phases should reflect trends in their confidence.

How sure were subjects of their rankings, and how did this confidence change? Even on first presentation of the principles, subjects exhibited a considerable degree of confidence. Only 19 percent were unsure or very unsure. Roughly 65 percent indicated that they were either sure or very sure.[5] Table 12 shows how subjects' confidence in their rankings increased over the period prior to the group decision and discussion. The center column indicates all individuals whose confidence neither rose nor fell during the first part of the experiment. Each other column represents a rise (to the right) or a drop (to the left) of one unit on the scale. In summary, 57 individuals show a decrease in their confidence, while 135 show an increase, for a net gain of 78 individuals exhibiting more certainty. These changes result in a profile of considerable confidence. After the first phase, only 51 individuals are unsure or very unsure (down

5. Additional tests (not shown) indicate that the differences in confidence in rankings did not vary significantly as a function of which principle was preferred.

Table 12. Changes in Subjects' Confidence in Rankings prior to Discussion

Number of subjects: 472

Mean score for degree of confidence

First measure: 3.52   F 33.36
Second measure: 3.77   p .001

First Measure	Losses in Degrees of Confidence				No Change	Gains in Degrees of Confidence				Net Changes
	4	3	2	1		1	2	3	4	
Very unsure					2	2	2	0	1	5
Unsure				-4	23	17	37	4		54
No opinion				-5	29	36	1			32
Sure		-1	-14	-23	198	35				-3
Very sure	0	0	0	-10	28					-10
Total	0	-1	-14	-42	280	90	40	4	1	78
Percent of 472	0	0	3	9	59	19	8	1	0	16

from 94), while 353 are sure or very sure.[6] And the overall shift toward more confidence is statistically significant (as shown by the *F*-test performed on the two mean confidence-level scores). These shifts were brought about by the activities in the first part of the experiment. Subjects read about the principles in their handbooks and made individual choices that affected their private earnings. It appears that these experiences caused considerable gross movement, led increasing numbers of people to prefer the principle of maximum income, led to a relatively large and loyal set of supporters for the floor-constraint principle, and increased the subjects' conviction in their rankings.

Changes during the Discussion and Decision

The next phase of the experiments consisted of group discussion and selection of a principle of distributive justice to govern the subsequent payoffs.[7] This phase is the heart of the process. At this point impartial reasoning is presumed to be invoked. Thus, if the experiments are to be effective, we would expect to see considerable changes in preferences in principles or, at the minimum, considerable firming of the confidence of the subjects in their expressed preferences over this phase.

Let us begin by looking at the impact of discussion and decision on subjects' preferences. Rows 1 and 2 in Table 13 present first-place rankings prior to and after the decision phase.

6. The rows represent the subjects' initial levels of confidence. To determine the prediscussion level of confidence one must look along the NE/SW diagonals. For example, the number who are very unsure at the prediscussion measure are all those who initially were very unsure and did not change (two) plus those who were initially unsure and lost 1 degree of confidence (four) (the −4 to the left and below the first 1 in the first row) plus one who was initially sure but became very unsure. Thus the total number is seven.

7. In most experimental groups, the subjects were to discuss the principles on the agenda and to select a principle unanimously. The selection was to be made after they unanimously agreed that their discussion need proceed no farther. We used three variants to these procedures. But, to preserve simplicity, the results reported in the next tables aggregate all types of experiments in which the group made a choice of principle. Filtering out the other cases does not change the analysis.

Table 13. Shifts in Individuals' First-Place Rankings of Principles over the Time of Decision

	Maximum Floor	Maximum Income	Floor Constraint	Range Constraint	Total
1. Prior to decision	29	105	236	39	409
2. After decision	17	77	287	28	409
3. Net changes	*-12*	*-28*	*51*	*-11*	0
4. Gross gains	5	12	65	11	93
5. Gross losses	-17	-40	-14	-22	-93
6. Desertion rate (line 5 / line 1)	.59	.38	.06	.57	.23

Row 3 (the difference between rows 1 and 2) shows the net changes in first-place rankings of the principles over the course of the discussion and decision. As we would expect, the floor constraint gained considerable first-place rankings (51). At that point in the experiment it was preeminent: it received 287 of 409 possible first-place rankings. The floor constraint's gain of first-place rankings came at the expense of each of the other principles, which lost between one-quarter and two-fifths of their first-place rankings. This time maximum income, the big gainer prior to the discussions, was the big loser. Its losses more than wiped out its previous gains. And the fifty-one net changes for the floor constraint reflect even more movement. In all, ninety-three subjects (23 percent) changed their first choice of principles over this portion of the experiment.

But do these changes in preference represent growing insecurity or growing confidence in the subjects? Only if their confidence grew would the discussion and decision be evidence of a trend toward a reflective equilibrium. The discussion appears to have had a positive impact on the subjects' convictions. The data in Table 14 show an apparent firming in subjects' confidence levels. The next to last row of the table shows the totals of shifts in confidence. Overall 132 individuals indicate a change in their confidence levels. Thirty-two persons were less confident and 100 more: a net gain of 68. Of the 413 subjects responding to both sets of questions, 350, or 85 percent (up from 311), were either sure or very sure of their response by the time the group choice has been made. Only 26, or 6 percent (down from 39), were unsure or very unsure. And the net change in confidence is highly significant (at the .001 level) as is evident in the F-test of average confidence scores.

Overall Changes Caused by the Experiment

Taken together, the shifts in both preference and confidence are clear evidence of considerable movement caused by both the learning and decision phases. This finding reinforces our conviction that the experimental structure itself has an impact on subjects' preferences.

Table 14. Changes in Subjects' Confidence in Rankings over the Time of Discussion

Number of subjects   413

Mean score for degree of confidence

Second measure 3.79 F 19.39

Third measure 3.97 p .001

First Measure	Losses in Degrees of Confidence				No Change	Gains in Degrees of Confidence				Net Changes
	4	3	2	1		1	2	3	4	
Very unsure				-0	2	1	2	0	1	4
Unsure				-3	7	6	19	1		26
No opinion			-1	-5	22	35	2			33
Sure		-2	-8	-9	205	33				18
Very sure	-2	0	-2	-9	45					-13
Total	-2	-2	-11	-17	281	75	23	1	1	68
Percent of 413	1	1	3	4	68	18	6	0	0	16

The tabular results can be put into graph form to demonstrate the impact of each phase. The net support for the principles is depicted in Figure 7. In that graph it becomes clear that
the floor constraint has no peer. It not only starts strong, it, and
only it, never loses net support. And in the end the discussion
generates even broader support for the floor-constraint principle. In other words, the preponderance of group choices of a
floor constraint reflects individuals' stated preferences.

Principles other than the floor constraint had a relatively
low percentage of loyal supporters. So, for example, during the
discussion, the floor maximizers and the range supporters had
defection rates of 59 percent and 57 percent, respectively. Even
a high percentage of the groups supporting maximum income
were disloyal: a defection rate of 38 percent. By contrast, the
floor-constraint supporters were 94 percent loyal. They are the
only group who were more loyal during the discussion than
they were during the first phase. Supporters of other principles
had increased levels of desertion during the discussion, as is
shown graphically in Figure 8. There it is apparent that the
floor-constraint principle is the only one to have fewer deser-
tions as time goes on. The unique loyalty of its supporters lets
it gain a robust support base relative to all the other principles.
Indeed, its desertion rate, in the second part of the experiment,
is less than one-sixth that of the most stably supported other
principle!

THE EFFECT OF IMPOSING PRINCIPLES

We have direct evidence that the discussion and participation
in a group decision have an impact on subjects' preferences. Yet
doubts may remain. Other factors could be at work. For example, what about the effect of experimenter influence? Were
subtle cues somehow transmitted to the subjects by the experimenters? Did subjects attempt to divine some presumably preferred principle, attempt to adjust their preferences accordingly,
and choose it? Recall that in one subset of the experiments,

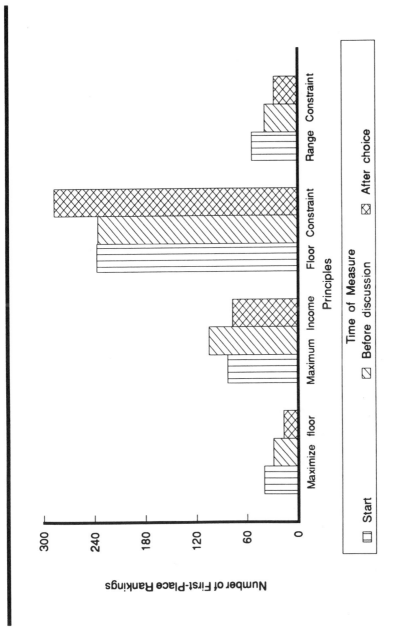

Figure 7. First-Place Rankings at Three Successive Points in the Experiment

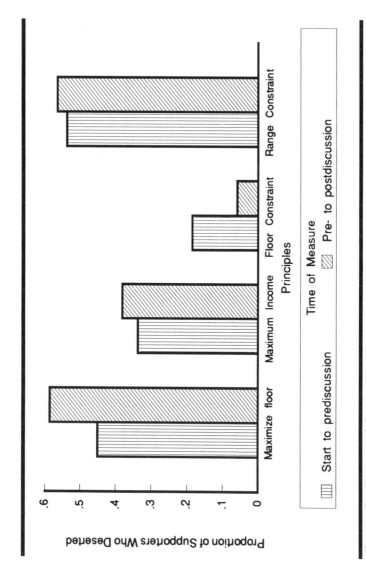

Figure 8. Rates of Desertion from Principles over the Course of the Experiments

subjects did not discuss and choose principles. The experimenters announced the principle that was to govern the final payoffs. The imposed principle was that of a floor constraint of $9,900. Measures of subjects' preferences before and after the imposition can be examined to see whether the impact of imposition on subjects' dispositions was different from that of discussion. If discussion and decision have a greater effect than imposition on changes in preferences and increases in confidence, that would be further evidence of the power of the experiments to generate a modicum of impartial reasoning.

The picture of changes of first-place rankings during the imposed experiments (Table 15) is clearly different from what we observed earlier (Table 11). In this experimental treatment there is no appreciable net change in first-place rankings of any principle. Without discussion and choice from an impartial point of view, subjects appear not to change their preferences. This basic conclusion is complemented by the data on changes in confidence. Without the discussion and choice, confidence in one's preferences does not increase over this period. Indeed, the shift is in the opposite direction (although it is not significant).[8]

LABORATORY CONDITIONS: POSSIBLE DISTURBING FACTORS

All this supportive evidence does not mean that the experiment is "clean" and that the results can be interpreted without further ado. Other factors were observed to affect group choices. The confinement of the decisions to a laboratory environment occasionally had a seriously distorting effect. And these distortions led to a certain degree of statistical dispersion around the most frequently predicted, or modal, choice.

For example, the idiosyncratic trajectory of a particular

8. The mean confidence score prior to imposition was 3.57. After imposition it had dropped to 3.45. The probability that this difference reflected no underlying difference is 0.4.

Table 15. Shifts in Individuals' First-Place Rankings of Principles over the Time of Imposition of Principle

	Maximum Floor	Maximum Income	Floor Constraint	Range Constraint	Total
1. Prior to decision	5	11	25	9	50
2. After decision	5	12	25	8	50
3. Net changes	*0*	*1*	*0*	*-1*	0
4. Gross gains	2	3	4	1	10
5. Gross losses	-2	-2	-4	-2	10
6. Desertion rate (line 5 / line 1)	.4	.25	.16	.13	.2

discussion appears to have been (on occasion) a factor bearing on the outcóme of the group decision. The pattern of the particular arguments advanced occasionally seems to have led to deviant results, which could explain why some groups chose a principle other than the floor constraint. Some impressionistic data are germane to this conjecture. In some experiments the discussions appear not to have been complete enough: they may not have evoked the relevant arguments; they may not have allowed the parties to reach a truly comfortable consensus; or they may have proceeded down the "wrong" path. An example of such an argument in a group that chose maximum income is instructive:

SUBJECT 1:   I'm not looking at it from an individual point of view. I'm looking at it as if I'm some kind of god. I'm looking down on what is best for society, not what is best for me. . . . I think the best thing is maximizing the average.

SUBJECT 2:   Well, think about it as if you might find yourself in any one of the given situations.

SUBJECT 1:   But that's not how I choose to look at it. If I was going to look at it this way, as an individual, then my first choice would be number 4 [setting a range constraint]. That way I would make sure that I was going to make at least this much. (*Transcripts*, p. 348)

The "god" made his perspective prevail, and the group choice in this case was maximum income, the main argument being utilitarian. But as one subject noted, "I just hope to hell I don't find myself on the bottom" (*Transcripts*, p. 350).

In another of the experiments in which the group's income was dependent on everyone's effort, an experimental-context argument was evoked:

SUBJECT 1:   With a range constraint of zero everyone gets the same.

SUBJECT 2:   We don't want everybody getting the same.

SUBJECT 3:   With the five of us here we can be a little more egalitarian than any other society because we can trust five people a lot more than we can trust fifty mil-

> lion. If there were fifty million of us, there's no way
> I'd agree to it. But if there are five of us, I'll agree to
> it.

SUBJECT 4: We all came in here with the same idea and none of
us knew what was going to be asked of us. So none
of us had a chance to be prepared or the opportunity
to be prepared by education or whatever. . . .

SUBJECT 5: If we all swore that we were going to put in our best
effort—

SUBJECT 1: Because you figure this isn't like a society where
you have to study hard and do this and this and then
you're going to be good and half of us study real
hard and half of us be lazy. It's not like that.

SUBJECT 5: We're all spending the same time in here. (*Transcripts*, p. 133)

And so, on the basis of that context-dependent argument, they
agreed to an egalitarian distribution where each would get one-
fifth of total production: a range constraint of zero. But they
were quite conscious of the fact that they would never choose
it for a larger society.

The conditions of impartial reasoning require not only a
separation of individual interests from specific assignments of
individuals to positions in society but also a full discussion in
which subjects reach a reflective equilibrium. Clearly the discussion in the laboratory cannot always achieve that ideal. The
quotes from the aberrant discussions are not the rule. Most discussions went smoothly without imaginary roles of god and
the like. Nor were many decisions motivated by the specific
conditions of the purely experimental environment. Nevertheless, some variance in outcomes might be expected to flow
from the peculiarities of particular discussions.

CONCLUSIONS

To support our contention that the floor-constraint principle
has a claim to ethical validity it is necessary to establish that
the experiments made a difference in subjects' preferences.
From the evidence, this appears to be the case. Participation in

the experiments made a difference in the subjects' evaluations of the principles. Their rankings changed over the course of the experiment. The choices of a floor constraint mirror underlying shifts in both individual preferences and increasing confidence in those preferences. The group choices do not appear to be a simple imposition of the majority's will on a minority. A discussion that involves the presumed invocation of impartial reasoning brings the principle of a floor constraint to the fore. The manner in which the decisions are made gives the principle a claim to ethical validity.

But it is one thing to agree that a principle is fair when you do not know how you fit into the overall scheme. It is quite another to live with the rule after finding out that you are among the most skilled, talented, and fortunate, or among the most disadvantaged. A rule that is seen as fair from an impartial point of view has a claim to ethical validity. But how would such a rule be received in practice? Would its ethical attractiveness pale as individuals experienced its redistributive impact? The next part of the book deals with that question.

PART III

Living with
Impartial Decisions

When you give people money, they don't want to do
things. And so if they're guaranteed it, they're not
going to go to work.
Transcripts (p. 235)

Okay, in maximizing the floor in real life—what
that's going to do is slow the incentive of the high
wage earners.
Transcripts (p. 211)

So the people that make the more money have to
support the people that don't do anything. . . .
That's not fair. . . . I should get what I worked [for]
and what I deserve. I don't think I should have to
pay for some bum.
Transcripts (p. 147)

We now have a good idea of what to expect when individuals
confront issues of distributive justice from an impartial point
of view. When individuals are ignorant of their particular interests, they can reach consensus and exhibit a great deal of consistency regarding their choices. The floor-constraint principle
gets widespread support.

But what happens after the decision? How do they feel about
this policy when they have to live with it? When ignorance dis-
sipates and they know their particular roles, how do they react
to a rule that ex ante appeared fair? After all, it is only then that
they experience the full consequences of the situation they
have created.

Philosophers such as Nozick (1974) have argued that entitlements play a major role in distributive justice. Nozick felt that any principle of justice that calls for particular patterns of income contravenes individual rights. He maintained that those who earn more because of their efforts, talents, and conditions of birth are entitled to keep their share of the wealth. Any redistribution of income away from them to others undermines support for the system. Those who are high producers will feel that they are not getting their due. At the same time the worst-off may begin to feel that they are being treated meanly. Support for the principle will erode, and the system will ultimately become unstable. This result is clearly problematic. If an impartial decision is to survive in practice, it must command allegiance. It cannot appear unfair once ignorance is replaced with knowledge. It cannot be too unpalatable in practice if it is to have ethical force. Preferences for justice must have some ex post stability.

But dissatisfaction with the consequences of the principle could lead to more than a simple decline of support. If productive members of society feel that the tax burden needed to support a floor income is too onerous, their incentives to work may be undercut, while those with a guaranteed income may relax their efforts to become self-sufficient. If redistribution leads to substantially decreased efforts and a radical decrease in productivity, then support for the principle might be expected to drop off. These arguments can be combined to generate what might be termed an *alienation hypothesis*, which we could adapt and state as:

> The satisfaction with the group's decision, made from an impartial point of view, will decline as subjects begin to experience redistribution.

The substance of the redistributive policy may be problematic, but the manner of its adoption may also matter. Specifically, individuals' allegiance to a policy could be a function of the procedure by which the policy was chosen. Thus, it could be that individuals relate positively to an incomes policy that they have chosen in an accepted democratic fashion. But they might object to the same policy were it imposed on them. Democratic mechanisms enjoy widespread popularity. Perhaps significant democratic participation in the political process lends legitimacy to policies and promotes stability of individual preferences.[1]

These three factors—the perceived fairness of redistribution in practice, the impact of redistribution on productivity, and the manner of adoption—bear directly on the survival of a redistributive policy. The issues of the policy's viability can be encapsulated in three questions:

1. Do individuals maintain their support for a principle of distributive justice when it is applied to the income they earn?
2. Is redistribution compatible with maintaining economic productivity?
3. Do democratic procedures and participation make a difference in subsequent attitudes and productive behavior?

To address these fundamental questions a series of experiments was run in which subjects did actual tasks for individual wages and then experienced redistribution of their earnings under a taxation scheme designed to implement a floor constraint. In one experimental treatment the redistributive policy was chosen by them from an impartial point of view. In the other it was imposed.[2] Analysis of subjects' evolving attitudes and production records allows us to furnish partial answers to the questions we have posed.

The procedure employed was straightforward. After the choice or imposition of a principle, all subjects earned money by correcting spelling mistakes in texts by Parsons.[3] Each indi-

1. Here we are concerned with the stability of individual preferences. The issue of cyclical majorities in democracies, although important, is not within the scope of this work or argument.

2. In most other respects these experiments resemble those reported on above; however, five of these groups were allowed to choose a principle by majority vote rather than by unanimity.

3. As we mentioned in Chapter 3, they did not know what the task would be prior to their choice of a principle. Because they did not know whether they would be paid on the basis of physical strength, agility, memory, mathematical ability, or some other talent, this uncertainty is presumed to have encouraged them to reason impartially.

vidual did the same task, and each received wages for his or her individual production (for a sample, see Table 4). The marginal pay rates (see Table 5) had considerable returns to scale. Individuals' outputs were checked, and their earnings and take-home pay were calculated and reported to them along with the equivalent yearly income flows implied by the earnings. The principle (either chosen or imposed) was then applied to their earnings. Taxes were levied and the redistribution was carried out. Their posttax payments for that period were calculated and reported to each of them. Taxes needed to raise individuals above the floor income were assessed proportionately against the earnings of those who earned more than the floor income.

This process of work, pay, and redistribution was repeated three times in each experiment. Measurements of the subjects' preferences for principles, satisfaction with the principles, and degree of certainty regarding their rankings were made after each tax transfer took place.[4] Repeating the task allowed for an examination of changes in the relationship between experience with redistribution and (1) attitudes toward the principles and (2) productivity. An analysis of the data from these experiments allows us to reach conclusions bearing on stability of preference and productivity.

In short, our conclusions are simple and encouraging. The answers to all three questions are affirmative. Support for the floor-constraint principle is firm when subjects experience it in practice. Moreover, productivity tends to increase rather than to decrease as subjects work and experience redistribution. Satisfaction shows an increasing trend, and alienation is not evident.

And democracy matters. In contrast with imposition of a principle, discussion and choice makes people more supportive of the principle, more secure in their preferences, more satisfied, and increasingly more productive. Productivity increases substantially among low producers, which decreases the need

---

4. Satisfaction with the choice of principle was measured only after the last production period in the imposed experiments.

for transfer payments dramatically. When there is no democratic choice, there are no such gains and no lowering of needed transfer payments. The gains in productivity are attributable to the impact of the discussion and choice, as well as to experience with the operation of the principle over time. They are not merely an artifact of participation in the group discussion and choice.

In Chapter 8 we analyze the question of stability and support in some detail by examining the impact of the income-redistribution system on the attitudes of the subjects. In Chapter 9 we investigate the relationship between the redistributive system and productivity.

CHAPTER EIGHT

Stability of Preferences
and Satisfaction
in a Working Environment

Individuals who must transfer income to others may not be happy with the redistributive policy; they may prefer less redistribution. Conversely those who get transfers may also be unhappy and may prefer a policy of more redistribution. Either the demand for less or the demand for more could undermine the stability of any redistributive policy.

RESEARCH QUESTIONS

Such significant erosion of support for a principle would undercut the importance of the finding that groups can agree on a principle from an impartial point of view. And if those who pay and those who receive show markedly different attitudes, this result might create factions and tensions that could undermine the policy. To determine the extent of such tendencies, the attitudes and preferences of taxpayers and recipients of transfer payments are examined and contrasted.

But our interest in stability is not limited to the impact of economic factors. We are also interested in whether democratic participation makes a difference. Does the actual discussion and choice affect attitudes? Do participants in democratic decisions differ in their subsequent attitudes from those who play no role? To answer these questions we track subjects' attitudes over the course of the experiment. We contrast the attitudes of those who helped choose the principle with the attitudes of those who had the floor constraint imposed by the experimenters.

All in all, we ran twenty-eight experiments in which subjects experienced three rounds of work, pay, and redistribution. In eighteen, groups chose the principle under which they were to labor, as in the experiments already discussed.[1] In the remaining ten, there was no discussion and no group choice. The experimenters imposed the redistributive principle. To examine the questions we have posed, eleven groups in which subjects chose the floor-constraint principle without qualifications are contrasted with the ten on whom we imposed a floor constraint.

The major findings can be summarized simply. First, support for the floor-constraint principle exhibits considerable stability. At both the beginning and the end of all production periods the floor constraint was by far the most popular principle. It was the most popular both when subjects chose it from an impartial point of view and when it was imposed by the experimenters. Both those who were taxed and those who received transfers maintained high levels of support for the principle; and their confidence in their rankings increased.

Second, that same stability is evident in individuals' satisfaction with the principle. Shifts occur, but they are not large or significant, although the trend is toward increasing satisfaction. But within those general parameters some relatively subtle experimental results emerge.

Third, democratic participation matters. Subjects who have a hand in choosing the principle are more confident in their choices and more satisfied, and their confidence grows in contrast with their counterparts who have a principle imposed on them.

1. In thirteen experiments unanimity was required for the adoption of a principle; in five majority rule was used.

But these summary conclusions follow from detailed consideration of the data. An appreciation of the magnitude of the effects requires a closer look.

RANKINGS OF PRINCIPLES

If experience with the floor-constraint principle leads to any drop in support, it should be evident as a drop in subjects' rankings of this principle after the three production periods. An examination of first-place rankings of principles and changes in first-place rankings reveals two things. (See Table 16.) The first we already know: the floor-constraint principle is an overwhelmingly popular principle and has more first-place rankings than all other principles combined: sixty-eight. Second, support for a floor constraint and for the other principles exhibits considerable net stability over the course of the production. At the end of all production and redistribution the floor-constraint principle has shown a small net loss of support: it has sixty-six first-place rankings. Thus, overall, experience with the floor-constraint principle appears not to undermine its basic popularity. When groups are broken down into those who chose democratically and those on whom the principle was imposed, this basic finding is maintained. The same is true for taxpayers and net recipients of transfers. There is no significant loss of first-place rankings in any of the groups in question.

CONFIDENCE IN RANKINGS OF PRINCIPLES

Stability of support for the floor-constraint principle is also evident in subjects' confidence in their preference rankings. Table 17 shows how subjects' confidence changed as they went through the production segments of the experiment. (Confidence was measured in the same way as described in Chapter 5, footnote 13.) The overall pattern is clear: none of the treatments led the subjects' conviction to lessen over time. Production, pay, taxes, and redistribution have a positive impact on

Table 16. Individuals' First-Place Rankings of Principles over the Course of Production ($\underline{N}$ = 105)

	First-Place Rankings after		Changes in First-Place Rankings		
	Choice or Imposition	Production	-	+	Net
Floor constraint	68	66	-6	4	-2
Range constraint	12	12	-2	2	0
Maximum income	20	24	-2	6	4
Maximizing the floor	5	3	-3	1	-2

Table 17. Impact of Production and Redistribution on Subjects' Confidence in Rankings

	Before Tasks	After Tasks	Differences	F	p
		All Experiments			
Number of subjects	120	119	119		
Mean	3.75	3.97	0.22	6.52	.012
Standard deviation	1.02	0.86			
		Unanimity Experiments			
Number of subjects	46	46	46		
Mean	3.84	4.26	0.42	9.02	.004
Standard deviation	0.99	0.57			
		Majority-Rule Experiments			
Number of subjects	25	24	24		
Mean	4.04	4.04	0.00	0.00	1.00
Standard deviation	0.55	0.62			
		Imposed-Principle Experiments			
Number of subjects	49	49	49		
Mean	3.51	3.67	0.16	1.03	.315
Standard deviation	1.17	1.07			

Note: Differences in Ns in any row and between columns are due to missing data.

Table 18. Effect of Discussion and Choice on Confidence in Rankings

	Imposed Means	Chosen Means	t	p
Before task 1	3.46	3.97	2.74	.077
Number of subjects	50	66		
After task 1	3.72	4.06	2.02	.045
Number of subjects	50	68		
After task 2	3.69	4.11	2.50	.014
Number of subjects	49	63		
After task 3	3.67	4.13	2.79	.006
Number of subjects	49	62		

Note: Differences in Ns in any column are due to missing data.

the certainty of subjects' rankings. But the different treatment groups show that trend in differing degrees. Only when the principle was chosen unanimously was the shift statistically significant. With unanimity, discussion and agreement seem to interact positively with the subjects' experience to reinforce their attitudes. Without consensus, discussion and agreement plus experience do not seem to have the same impact. Thus, unanimity seems to be the catalyst that generates the effect.[2]

Participation in the choice affects not only growth in conviction but also subjects' absolute levels of confidence in their rankings. Table 18 shows this effect. As the first line shows, subjects who participated in democratic decisions initially had only a marginally significant (at a .077 level) higher level of confidence. As the experiment proceeded, however, the differences grew and became increasingly significant. At the end,

2. These results also show up when we perform a parallel analysis for those subjects who were net taxpayers and those who were net recipients of transfers.

Table 19. Satisfaction after Gaining Knowledge of Self-
    Interest (N̲ = 140)

	Before Task 1	*After Task 1*	*After Task 2*	*After Task 3*
Mean	3.80	3.84	3.85	3.85
Number of subjects	94	93	97	125

Note: Differences in N̲s are due to missing data.

differences in the two confidence levels were significant at the
.006 level. Participating in the group choice (self-governance)
increased the confidence subjects had in their rankings as they
experienced the effect of their choice through income redistribution. Their conviction was reinforced rather than being undermined.

SATISFACTION WITH THE PRINCIPLE

Subjects' self-reported satisfaction with the floor-constraint
principle furnishes yet another measure of the stability of support. Specifically, we asked subjects before each production period and then after the last one how satisfied they were with
the principle.[3] Data from their responses can be used to translate the concerns of such philosophers as Nozick into falsifiable conjectures. Do the subjects evidence alienation over time
as they experience redistribution?

What do the data show? Table 19 reports the average levels of
satisfaction with the principle in each of the three production
periods. The aggregate data not only fail to support the alienation hypothesis but bolster the converse: increasing acceptabil-

3. The exact question read: "How satisfied are you with the distributive
principle selected by (for) the group? [Choose one of the following:] (a) very unsatisfied, (b) unsatisfied, (c) neither satisfied nor unsatisfied, (d) satisfied, (e) very
satisfied." Satisfaction was then scored 1–5, where 1 was very unsatisfied and 5
was very satisfied.

ity. Overall satisfaction rises steadily (although not steeply or significantly) over the production periods.

However, this overall positive trend could mask underlying instability. If a large number of subjects were increasing their satisfaction and many others were decreasing theirs, analysis of means would fail to reveal these fluctuations. High numbers of shifts would undermine the argument that satisfaction was stable. Data on changes in levels of satisfaction are reassuring in this regard. Of the 101 persons in the experiments with enough nonmissing data to be able to make the calculations, 58 never changed their level of satisfaction; 4 others, who made changes, eventually ended up back where they began.[4] Another 21 individuals ended up more satisfied than they had been before production began, including 3 who, although they became somewhat alienated during the course of the experiments, came to support the principle more at the end than at the beginning. However, 18 subjects had a lower degree of satisfaction at the end than they had at the beginning. In other words, a few more individuals were more satisfied at the end than they were at the beginning. This result lends further evidence to the notion that alienation does not increase when individuals experience the rule's impact on "real-life" earnings.[5]

DEMOCRATIC PARTICIPATION AND SATISFACTION

The data presented so far show that there is not much aggregate support for the alienation hypothesis. Still one wonders why

4. We count as never changing those who never changed their answer. Of these, one always responded with "very unsatisfied," three with "unsatisfied," fifteen with "neither satisfied nor unsatisfied," twenty-six with "satisfied," and thirteen with "very satisfied." Hardly a response of continuing or increasing dissatisfaction!

5. An attempt to identify the typical path of individual levels of satisfaction also fails. Such an attempt would require that the points on which we measured satisfaction (over the sequence of production periods) form a (unidimensional) scale. Although such a scaling test leads to very low stress measures ($r^2 >$ .9995), the order of the points on the scale conforms with neither the alienation hypothesis nor its inverse. Satisfaction does not increase monotonically.

Table 20. The Effect of Imposition versus Choice and Discussion on Satisfaction ($\underline{N} = 135$)

	Imposed Means	Chosen Means	t	p
Before task 1	3.33	3.94	2.37	.021
Number of subjects	15	64		
After task 1	3.40	3.97	2.56	.013
Number of subjects	15	63		
After task 2	3.33	3.97	2.30	.024
Number of subjects	15	67		
After task 3	3.60	3.90	1.56	.121
Number of subjects	42	68		

Note: Differences in $\underline{N}$s in any column are due to missing data.

not. Democratic participation furnishes one possible explanatory factor. We conjectured that satisfaction would be a function of democracy. Imposition of a principle was expected to evoke lower levels of satisfaction with the principle.[6]

The data in Table 20 attest to the importance of democratic choice.[7] Here, we compare subjects in the imposed experiments with subjects in choice experiments.[8] Where there is no discussion and choice, subjects are less satisfied with the principle. And the difference is quite significant especially over the first two task periods. But after the third task, the differences

6. Recall that two factors were different in the imposed experiments: discussion as well as choice was precluded.

7. Unfortunately all measures of satisfaction except for the final measure were omitted in most of the imposed-principle experiments and so the comparative analysis as a function of choice is not very solid using this variable. Still, notice that at the bottom of Table 21 the magnitudes of the differences in related variables would buttress the conjecture that the effect is quite significant.

8. We look only at those in groups that chose the floor constraint principle (so as to ensure comparability with the imposed principle).

fade into insignificance thanks largely to a gain in satisfaction among the imposed-experiment subjects. Apparently three periods of experience with the floor-constraint principle (which they had no part in choosing) was sufficiently positive to raise their satisfaction levels significantly. One other conclusion can be drawn from the data in the table. In neither group was the net change in subjects' levels of satisfaction (over the production experience) significant.

SATISFACTION AND THE INDIVIDUAL'S ECONOMIC EXPERIENCE

The other variable that might be expected to affect satisfaction is economic experience with redistribution. After all, this would seem to be the heart of the alienation hypothesis. Those who lose money in taxes might well react differently from those who gain via transfer payments. Table 21 gives the results of the comparison when we divide the subjects into those who were net taxpayers and those who were net recipients over the course of the experiments.[9] Note, both taxpayers and transfer recipients have a higher level of satisfaction at the end of the production periods than they do at the beginning. There is no evidence for alienation in either group. Initially, taxpayers are significantly (at the .05 level) more satisfied with the principle than recipients. But the differences are not large. Over the course of the experiment, as subjects experience the effects of redistribution, some fluidity in satisfaction becomes evident, and at one stage recipients are even more satisfied than taxpayers. But by the end of the experiment the initial order is reestablished, with a smaller (and less significant) gap in satisfaction between taxpayers and recipients than at the outset.[10] In

9. Other methods of characterizing taxpayers and recipients lead to similar conclusions. Five persons, all in the same experiment, neither paid taxes nor received benefits. The experiment was one in which the chosen principle was imposed and the production by all individuals was so high as to obviate the need for redistribution. These five persons are excluded from the analysis.

10. When results from only the choice experiments are considered, the initial difference in satisfaction between recipients and taxpayers (3.64 versus

Table 21. Satisfaction as a Function of Taxpaying Experience
($\underline{N} = 135$)

	Recipients		*Taxpayers*			
	Means	*N*	*Means*	*N*	*t*	*p*
Before task 1	3.57	42	3.98	47	1.99	.050
After task 1	3.83	41	3.85	47	0.11	.910
After task 2	3.91	44	3.81	48	0.48	.631
After task 3	3.71	56	4.00	64	1.70	.092
Total change from before task 1	0.14	34	0.02	43	1.71	.091

Notes: Differences in $\underline{N}$s in any column are due to missing data.

all, the data furnish no support for an alienation hypothesis and no major divergence in satisfaction between taxpayers and recipients after their experience with redistribution.

CONCLUSIONS

The analyses of the experimental data offer tentative answers to the questions regarding stability. The floor-constraint principle bears up well under use. There is no support for an alienation hypothesis. Subjects continue to rank a floor-constraint principle highly. Its first-place ranking is unchallenged. It is the principle of choice both before and after the production periods. Subjects are both more confident in their rankings as a result of their experience and are marginally more satisfied.

As might be expected, the procedure for choosing a principle

4.09, $t = 2.14$, $p = .036$) is reduced to insignificance by the end of the experiments (3.87 versus 4.07, $t = 0.947$, $p = .346$). Thus in the imposed experiments there are marginally greater differences in satisfaction between taxpayers and recipients than in the choice experiments.

makes a difference in subjects' attitudes, at least with regard to confidence. Those who are allowed a democratic choice are more confident in their rankings of the principles than those who are not given such a choice, and the confidence of those given a choice grows. They are more secure about their rankings after production and redistribution than they were before, especially when unanimity is required.[11] Democratic participation also leads to increased satisfaction with the redistributive policy.

Differences between the subjects' economic experience with the redistributive policy also fail to introduce a source of dissatisfaction. Taxpayers do not show lower levels of satisfaction than recipients. There is no evidence that those who pay feel hard done by. Nor do they show a diminished level of satisfaction. No feelings of entitlement to their earned income appear to undermine their support for redistribution in accordance with the principle.

In short, acceptance of the principle, if anything, is enhanced by the production and redistribution experience. There is no evidence of significant alienation. But these effects are stronger in the choice than in the imposed experiments. Participation in discussion and choice makes a difference in subsequent attitudes and changes in attitudes.

There is, of course, an alternative explanation to the positive role of participation in the decision process. Perhaps the discussion phase simply created group solidarity and a degree of interacting utility. Perhaps the gains are due to this newly generated esprit de corps rather than to the combined effects of the principle and participation in the selection process. But further patterns in the data lead us to believe that factors other than mere discussion are responsible for the differential behavior of subjects in the two treatment groups. What these factors are will be discussed in the next chapter.

11. Individuals in groups that reached decision by majority rule exhibit no significant change in the strength of their convictions. The same is true of subjects in the imposed-rule experiments.

CHAPTER NINE

Redistribution
and Productivity

Although the evidence in the previous chapter shows that subjects do not express alienation from the redistributive policy
when they experience it, the issue is not settled. Long-term
support for the policy can still be undermined if redistribution
has a negative impact on productivity. Over time, the prospects
for a policy that generates a shrinking pie are not encouraging.
In this chapter, we examine productivity under redistribution.
Again both the effects of democratic participation as well as the
subject's status as either taxpayer or transfer recipient are examined.

The data show that the redistributive policy does not have a
negative impact on production. Indeed, productivity increases,
despite the fact that at times the taxes and transfers are sizable.
The floor-constraint principle, in practice, does not appear,
generally, to dampen incentives. But the effects are not uniform. The worst-off show the greatest gains in productivity.
And when the principle is imposed, no significant gains in productivity are observed. The details of these findings cast light
on the questions we have posed.

Table 22. Overall Impact of Production Experience on Productivity

Subset of Subjects	First-Period Mean	Last-Period Mean	F	p	N
All experiments	5.78	6.65	9.87	.002	135
Choice experiments	5.82	7.02	10.92	.001	85
Imposed-rule experiments	5.70	6.02	0.58	.451	50

IMPACT OF DEMOCRACY AND EXPERIENCE
WITH REDISTRIBUTION ON PRODUCTIVITY

How, exactly, is productivity affected by experience with work and the distributive principle? Are such effects a function of the group's procedures for adopting the policy? The basic measure of productivity is the actual number of mistakes found and corrected by subjects at each of the three production phases. Changes in productivity using these measures should point out any possible effects.

Consider Table 22. It is clear from the first line of the table that, for the full set of experiments, experience with production and redistribution increased productivity. Average production rose significantly between the first and last periods. This is in flat contradiction to the drop anticipated by an alienation effect. There is, however, at least one possible explanation that would save the hypothesis that redistribution, sapping incentives, leads to reduced productivity. Because the tasks performed were repeated with different texts, subjects' experience with the task might be expected to increase their productivity as they progress along a learning curve. After all, subjects might be expected to increase their efficiency as they become more familiar with the demands and mechanics of what they are to do.

However, the breakdown of the subjects into choice and imposed-treatment groups negates this explanation as a basis for the observed increase in productivity. The last two lines of the table show that the increase in productivity found in the

group as a whole is statistically significant only when democratic procedures are used to choose the policy. When subjects
did not choose their own rule, they experienced only a marginal, and statistically insignificant, increase in productivity.
Whatever effect experience may have on increasing productivity, it is vitiated by working under an imposed policy. Democratic choice appears to make a difference in subsequent performance.

We can get additional insight into the effect of democratic
procedures by comparing the first- and last-period productivity
in Table 23. The initial productivity of subjects in the two
groups was not significantly different. Apparently the acts of
discussing and choosing a rule had no immediate impact on
their outputs. However, the difference in average production between the two groups in the last period widened considerably.
It was eight times larger in the last period $(7.02 - 6.02 = 1.00)$
than in the first $(5.82 - 5.70 = 0.12)$ and the differences approach statistical significance $(p = .074)$. Thus the lack of democracy appears to have an impact on the productivity of subjects as a whole after the subjects experience the consequences
of working under the rule, but the effect appears not to be particularly strong.

IMPACT OF TAX STATUS ON PRODUCTIVITY

Democracy (versus imposition) appears to have a moderate impact on productivity. What other variables affect productivity?
Is the performance of those in one subgroup more affected by
their experience than the performance of those in another
subgroup? Specifically, is the effect of experience different on
taxpayer than on transfer recipient?

When subjects are grouped as net taxpayers or net recipients
of transfers (over the whole experiment), some significant patterns emerge.[1] Not only are absolute levels of productivity af-

1. It should be noted that other ways of implementing the concept of taxpayer status do not lead to more than marginal changes in the conclusions supported by the data analysis.

Table 23. Impact of Choice versus Imposition on Productivity ($\underline{N} = 135$)

	Choice-Experiment Mean	Imposed-Experiment Mean	F	p
First production	5.82	5.70	0.04	.852
Last production	7.02	6.02	3.24	.074

Table 24. Impact of Tax-Status Changes on Productivity: All Experiments

	First-Period Mean	Last-Period Mean	F	p	N
Taxpayers' production	7.51	8.23	4.08	.047	71
Share per capita	0.27	0.25	1.45	.232	71
Recipients' production	3.49	4.58	5.35	.024	59
Share per capita	0.12	0.14	1.60	.211	59

fected, but relative productivity of the two groups varies as well. To show this effect, we calculate the contribution of each individual to the group's production in both the first and last periods. Note that equally productive individuals would each produce 0.2 of the group's output. We then compare the average share of the group's production by taxpayers and by transfer recipients. Changes in this statistic should reflect changes in the relative productivity of taxpayers and recipients over the course of the experiments.

The data in Table 24 indicate that, in the experiment as a whole, whether a subject is a taxpayer or not, productivity appears to rise, although recipients' production appears to rise more sharply than taxpayers'. Moreover, there is no apparent significant difference in the share of burdens borne by taxpayers and recipients over the course of the experiments. The relative

Table 25. Impact of Experimental Treatment and Tax Status on Productivity

	First-Period Mean	Last-Period Mean	F	p	N
	Choice Experiments				
Taxpayers' production	7.51	8.32	3.11	.084	47
Share per capita	0.27	0.23	4.86	.033	47
Recipients' production	3.66	5.42	8.17	.007	38
Share per capita	0.12	0.16	4.48	.041	38
	Imposed Experiments				
Taxpayers' production	7.52	8.17	1.35	.255	29
Share per capita	0.26	0.27	0.35	.558	29
Recipients' production	3.20	3.05	0.05	.824	21
Share per capita	0.13	0.10	0.79	.385	21

contributions of these subgroups to production are fairly stable between the first and last period.

IMPACT OF TAX STATUS AND POLICY-ADOPTION
PROCEDURES ON PRODUCTIVITY

We know that the way in which the redistribution policy is adopted makes a difference in subsequent productivity. Tax status appears not to make a difference. It remains to be seen whether the effect of democratic participation interacts with tax status. In other words, do taxpayers and recipients behave differently in democratic contexts than in imposed regimes? Table 25 shows strong interactive effects. When subjects chose their principle, there was an increase in productivity among both taxpayers and recipients. But transfer recipients increased their productivity quite dramatically. The gain was highly significant both substantively and statistically. Corrections were almost 50 percent higher (statistically significant at the .007 level). The gain was lower among taxpayers. For taxpayers the increase in corrections was only 10 percent ($p = .084$). This differential increase in productivity between the two groups reflects an increased share of the groups' production accomplished by transfer recipients over the course of the experiment. Their per capita share of production rose significantly, from 12 percent during the first period to 16 percent during the last (a 35 percent increase). In other words, recipients became relatively more productive members of their experimental group as time went on.

The picture in the imposed experiments is quite different. There, taxpayers increased their production, but the increase was statistically insignificant. Recipients show a small, and statistically insignificant, drop in productivity.[2] These small changes lead to no significant change in the share produced by the two groups, although the recipients diminish their relative contribution slightly.

Thus policy-adoption procedures and tax status interacted to produce striking differences in the behavior of the four groups. As time passed, low-producing subjects in the two treatment groups reacted differently to their experiences with the redistributional system. The strength and significance of those differences are shown directly in Table 26.

The impact of self-governance is clear and unequivocal. Transfer recipients who were in groups that chose their own principles outperformed their counterparts in groups with imposed policies by a wide and significant margin. They produced, on average, 2.37 more corrections, or 77 percent more ($p = .002$). Recipients in the choice groups increased their productivity not only in absolute terms but also relative to the taxpayers in their groups. Thus they account for a larger share

2. One possible explanation for the greater increase in productivity of recipients in the choice experiments is that the taxpayers were already producing at such a high rate that there was little room for improvement. That explanation is negated by the finding that in the imposed experiments the productivity of the taxpayers increased while that of the recipients decreased.

Table 26. Impact of Choice versus Imposition on Final Production by Tax Status

	Choice-Experiment Mean	Imposed-Experiment Mean	F	p	N
Recipients' last production	5.42	3.05	10.43	.002	59
Share per capita	0.16	0.10	7.04	.010	59
Taxpayers' last production	8.32	8.17	0.22	.641	76
Share per capita	0.23	0.27	7.68	.007	76

of their group's production: their production ratio is 60 percent higher than that of their counterparts in the imposed experiments ($p = .01$).

The effect of democracy on taxpayers is a different matter. Indeed, it had no significant effect on their performance. The average taxpayer contributed a lower share to the total production (23.7 percent) in groups with choice than did counterparts in the groups with no choice (26.9 percent). But this difference is fully attributable to the increase in productivity of recipients in the choice experiments. Figure 9 portrays these differences in another way.

Because the choice groups also engaged in discussions about the policy issue, one might believe that these effects stemmed from mere discussion. After all, discussion might engender group solidarity and lead to increased efforts. But the data contain evidence to negate this possible explanation. There was no significant difference in the initial measures of productivity for either recipients or taxpayers across treatment groups.[3] Thus, the improved performance among recipients in the choice experiments cannot be attributed solely to a discussion effect. It emerges only after subjects have experienced production and redistribution.

Moreover, the choice/imposition distinction does not act uniformly on the classes created by the redistribution policy. The content of the decision and the status of the subjects in the environment after they ascertain their economic status make a difference. These two observations—initial lack of difference and subsequent large differences only for transfer recipients— give further force to the argument that the observed differences are not due solely to participation. They are a product of an interaction of democratic choice and the individual's status under the implementation of the redistributive principle.

---

3. The F-statistic for the effect of experimental treatment on recipients' productivity is minuscule for the first round of production ($F = 0.392$, significant at the .534 level). For taxpayers it is vanishingly small.

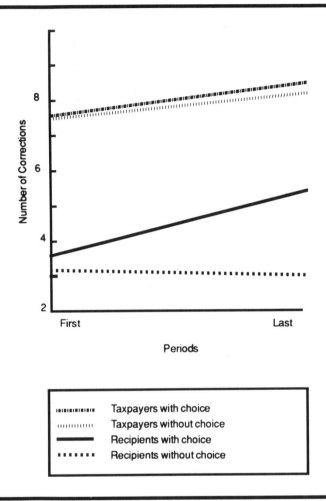

Figure 9. Democratic Choice, Tax Status, and Changes in Productivity

IMPACT OF AGREEMENT AND DISSENT
ON PRODUCTIVITY

When the experiments required unanimous agreement on a principle, some subjects had to compromise. Although all experimental groups charged with reaching consensus on a principle did so, some individuals in each group did not get their first choice. In each group, at least one subject did not rank the chosen (or imposed) principle first. One wonders, therefore, how agreement with, as opposed to dissent from, the group's chosen principle affected the subjects' productivity. Did those who preferred the principles that the groups chose show higher levels of productivity?

If the content of the group choice (rather than the simple fact of making a choice or having one imposed) is important in determining subsequent behavior, one should expect to find dissenters performing more poorly than those who assented. To test for this possibility subjects were categorized into two groups: those who favored the operative principle and those who favored a different principle. This categorization was operationalized by examining subjects' reported preferences for principles just after the group choice (or imposition).[4]

As shown in Table 27, agreement with the principle did not significantly affect the productivity of subjects in the first round of production.[5] The average number of corrections found by the subjects who agreed with the principle was not significantly different from that of those who dissented (5.4 versus 5.2). But an effect does emerge over time. By the final round the production of those who agreed became significantly higher than that of those who disagreed (6.9 versus 5.0, significant at the .005 level). Those who agreed increased their production

4. Only groups choosing the principle of floor constraint without qualification were included in this analysis so that they could be compared unambiguously with the group on whom the principle was imposed.

5. Those who ranked the governing principle as their own most-preferred principle are labeled "agree" and contrasted with those preferring a different principle (labeled "disagree").

Table 27. Impact of Agreement and Dissent on Productivity (N = 100)

| | Means for Those Who | | | |
	Agree (N = 66)	Disagree (N = 34)	F	p
First production	5.42	5.24	0.07	.798
Last production	6.92	5.03	8.30	.005
Change in production	1.50	-0.22	6.18	.015

significantly, while dissenters reduced theirs marginally. Agreement with the principle under which one works has an effect on productivity.

Given the differential impact of the experimental treatment on taxpayers and recipients that we noted previously, the subjects were further categorized by tax status, and separate analyses were performed on recipients and taxpayers. Those results are presented in Table 28. An analysis of the effect of agreement yields results similar to the analysis of democratic choice. As with previous effects, no differences were found between the groups in the first round. In the last round, however, significant differences were apparent. In the final production stage, transfer recipients who agreed with the principle had significantly higher production than their counterparts who did not: 4.9 corrections versus 2.7, a difference of almost 80 percent (significant at $p = .02$). These differences resulted in a change in productivity that was on average positive for assentors ($+2.4$) and negative for dissenters (-0.6, significant at the .013 level). And these changes led to differences in the proportions of the overall share of production borne by the two groups. By the end recipients who agreed with their rule on average produced 16 percent of their group's output, while those who dissented produced a paltry 9 percent.

But in this case taxpayers also seemed to be affected by whether they agreed or disagreed with the principle governing their final income. Those who agreed showed insignificantly higher levels of production in the first round than those who did not. By the last period that gap had spread to 8.5 versus 6.8 ($p = .01$), with taxpayers who agreed more productive than those who did not.[6]

Finally, a regression analysis reveals that combining discussion and agreement with the governing principle yields considerable explanatory power. Together, for recipients, these two variables account for 20 percent of the observed production

6. Because they also began with marginally higher levels of productivity than their dissenting counterparts, their changes neither in productivity nor in the relative share of production are significant.

Table 28. Impact of Agreement and Dissent on Productivity by Tax Status

	Means for Those Who			
	Agree (N = 66)	Disagree (N = 34)	F	p
Recipients (N = 44)				
First production	2.55	3.33	0.95	.335
Last production	4.90	2.73	5.86	.020
Change in production	2.35	-0.60	6.69	.013
Share per capita: first production	0.09	0.11	0.35	.560
Share per capita: last production	0.16	0.09	7.00	.011
Taxpayers (N = 56)				
First production	7.68	6.74	1.51	.225
Last production	8.51	6.84	7.13	.010
Change in production	0.84	0.11	0.80	.376
Share per capita: first production	0.28	0.26	0.49	.488
Share per capita: last production	0.26	0.24	0.96	.330

variance in the last round. Among taxpayers, agreement alone explains just a bit less (14 percent).

CONCLUSIONS

The changes in productivity furnish texture and color to our fabric. On the basis of these results we can now also offer tentative answers to the questions we posed about productivity and stability. The predicted conflict between distributive justice and productivity did not materialize. Productivity was affected by the redistributive policy, but the effect was not uniform. Differences in the impact of redistribution were a function of how the policy came to be adopted. Indeed, rather than being reduced, productivity was increased when the policy was arrived at in a participatory, democratic fashion.

When there was democratic choice, there was a strong and clear positive gain in productivity over the course of the experiments. Without it, there was no significant rise in productivity. *Participation in discussions of taxation and input into the choice of a rule to govern redistribution have a clear and positive impact on subsequent productivity.* Participatory democracy (at least in an experimental setting) aids productivity.

But even this effect is not uniform. The effect is more pronounced for those who benefit from income transfers. When agreed to in a participative fashion, the taxation and redistribution system that guarantees a floor acts as an incentive to those at the bottom of the income distribution. Those who pay taxes also do not diminish their output. Rather they show a trend toward increased productivity. The record of those who worked under an imposed policy is different. For them, the trend in production was downward, giving further impetus to the notion that participatory democracy as operationalized under conditions of impartiality can make a difference in subsequent behavior.

Nor is there evidence that group discussion alone engendered some form of group solidarity that generated the effects. The results offer evidence to the contrary: the observed effects do not seem to be a result of discussion per se. If the effects came from group solidarity generated by discussion, one would expect the greatest differences immediately after the discussion. This was not the case. Subjects in groups with and without discussion performed similarly in the first round of production. Only after they experienced the redistribution did their behavior begin to diverge. Discussion and choice were not enough to change behavior; discussion and choice, in combination with experience of the policy, were.

Further evidence that the effects were not an artifact is offered by the differential impact on taxpayers and recipients. If the observed effect was the product of discussion alone, one would have expected to find it in both taxpayers and transfer recipients. This was not the case. Taxpayers might not be expected to show a significant increase in productivity because of their diminished potential for improvement. After all, they are high producers already. The evidence shows, however, that taxpayers who agreed with the principle had significantly higher levels of production in the last phase of the experiment than those who disagreed. This evidence does much to negate a possible conjecture that maximum levels of productivity had been reached by taxpayers in the first round.

Finally, an examination of the actual preferences for principles among subjects and the effects of agreement on behavior offers further evidence for the internal validity of the results. Agreement with the principle affected final production in both tax-status groups. The content of the decision matters, not merely the manner in which it is reached. But the results are, in general, quite optimistic. They indicate that under reasonable conditions individuals are capable and exhibit a sense of social responsibility; they do not just free ride. This sense of responsibility would appear to be an important potential element in stabilizing the policies that engender distributive justice. In the words of Amartya Sen (1990, p. 54):

> If individuals do, in fact, incessantly and uncompromisingly advance only their narrow self-interests, then the pursuit of justice

will be hampered at every step by the opposition of everyone who has something to lose from any proposed change. If, on the other hand, individuals as social persons have broader values and objectives, including sympathy for others and commitment to ethical norms, then the promotion of social justice need not face unremitting opposition at every move.

PART IV

Conclusions

There is a property common to almost all the
moral sciences, and by which they are distin-
guished from many of the physical; that is, that it
is seldom in our power to make experiments in
them. . . . The consequence of this unavoidable de-
fect in the materials of the induction is, that we
can rarely obtain what Bacon has quaintly, but,
not unaptly, termed an *experimentum crusis.*
                    (Mill [1844] 1967, pp. 327–328)

CHAPTER TEN

Implications for Ethical Inquiry and Social Policy

The words of John Stuart Mill do not rule out the possibility of doing experiments in the moral sciences. Indeed, by asserting that one can seldom do experiments, he tacitly implies that sometimes one may. We have attempted to slip into that small opening hinted at almost 150 years ago. We do not claim that ours are crucial Baconian experiments; but they are a start. Being among the first of their genre, they are admittedly imperfect. Some of the implications of their imperfection are discussed in this chapter. Nevertheless, they provide some nonobvious, yet falsifiable, insights and are replicable. The importance of these shared properties, replicability and falsifiability, should be clear. These are properties shared with experiments in the natural sciences. They raise the possibility, and perhaps the promise, of cumulative progress in ethical matters.

AN EMPIRICAL METHODOLOGY FOR ETHICAL INQUIRY

What might one expect from an empirical methodology for ethical inquiry were it to succeed? Philosophers have built their search for ethical truths on the presumption that humanity can discover the nature of ethical truths via behavioral procedures such as reflection and introspection. Many of the disagreements among philosophers can be seen to be over three things: under what conditions, with what procedures, can which identifiable subset of humanity uncover these truths. Philosophers differ both as to which of these three elements they emphasize and as to how they substantively answer the questions to discover the good. But all scholars would argue that what is right or just is not to be measured simply by an opinion poll. For example, utilitarians such as R. M. Hare, Henry Sidgwick, and John Stuart Mill do not claim that everyone can reason well about ethical matters. For them, difficult moral issues cannot be decided by the common man. The way to discover the just is to ask those with the proper training to analyze the problem using the appropriate knowledge base. As pointed out previously, others, such as Rawls and Harsanyi, focus on the conditions under which the reasoning is to take place.

Using these three elements of ethical inquiry, we can fit our problem into the larger tradition. We have chosen as conditions those that support impartial reasoning. We have accepted the notion that it takes no special training or skill to explore ethical conditions. And we have, by our choice of procedure, made an epistemological choice: we have determined that the conclusions of our inquiry would take the form of testable conjectures. As such, they are meant to reorient the nature of ethical inquiry to more parallel that of science. One might say that the enterprise is to pursue truths via testable conjectures rather than to reveal truths via introspection.

If that project is reasonable, we now can begin to answer the fundamental question: What evidence must be brought to bear in understanding what is just? For us, the evidence is to be found in how humanity reasons about ethical matters. Our methods stem from the assumption that to understand some aspects of the good one must discover what people evaluate as good when they are in a position to reason impartially. Moreover, we believe that to obtain potentially cumulative knowledge about the results of impartial reasoning one must do empirical studies involving samples of humanity attempting to reason impartially. We assert that there must be an empirical link between the beliefs of humans and some aspects of the good.[1]And we take it as an article of faith, or a working hypothesis underlying our inquiry, that the beliefs of (the right) humans under these conditions could be homogeneous.

But the precise nature of the good does not necessarily follow in a straightforward fashion from this hypothesized positive link between the good and individuals' actual beliefs. It could be that what individuals believe to be morally right for single moral agents does not lead to collective justice. Indeed, the notion of collective justice (as in distributive matters) may require a collective judgment. Those conclusions may be quite different from what individual agents determine when thinking on their own, atomistically. Interactions among individuals who have divergent values and who are capable of judging tradeoffs when values conflict may be necessary to identify the content of distributive justice.

To find a common content, if it exists, we have to do more than conjecture about specific circumstances under which moral sentiments emerge. We have to identify the circumstances and then identify the content that emerges in those circumstances. In other words, we are looking for openings, or cracks, on some of the surfaces of ethical theorizing in which to insert an empirical wedge. We do not expect the leverage to come easily, nor to be fully generalizable. But judgments by both individuals and collectives are likely to be relevant to the questions posed.

CORRECTABLE AND TESTABLE CLAIMS IN ETHICS

In ethics, as in the natural sciences, both the empirically informed imagination of the theorist and careful empirical observation may lay the groundwork for a conjecture. However, the

1. This is not an uncontroversial position, and it flies in the face of some recent arguments in ethical theory. Some would hold that moral statements need not refer to an actual or contingent property of the world. So, for example, see Darwall's overview of the issues (1983, pp. 18–20) or Williams (1985, p. 153).

data collected to develop a set of conjectures are likely to be inadequate for testing their implications. New data, either naturally occurring or experimental, explicitly structured so as to reflect the theory, are required if the field is to be advanced. Thus, one of our main objectives is to begin the development of a methodology that will permit correctability of knowledge claims about some aspects of ethical matters.[2] If such a procedure is used in ethics, an onus will be shifted from ethical philosophers: they will no longer have to claim that bedrock or truth has been found.

As in other sciences, controlled tests of theoretical conjectures can certainly not lead to a discovery of what distributive justice is. After all, we do not know what time is or what copper is. We can define copper as some properties of protons, neutrons, and electrons constituted into an atom. And we can further define these subatomic particles by their smaller constituents, until we reach the current limits of our knowledge. But that process only characterizes copper in terms of other theoretical entities. As for time, the reduction cannot currently proceed.[3] We know it only in relation to other fundamental physical terms and constants. Uncertainties such as these are general in the physical sciences. The eminent philosopher Karl Popper (1959, p. 111) has written:

> The empirical basis of objective science has thus nothing "absolute" about it. Science does not rest upon rock-bottom. The bold structure of its theories rises, as it were, above a swamp. It is like

2. What we have in mind here is clearly different from a Rawlsian type of justification mechanism. Rawls suggested that we correct our "considered judgments" about morality via appeals to reasoning about principles. Specifically, we wish to discover something empirical about how individuals reason about, and groups choose from among, ethics and ethical principles under conditions that approximate the ideal conditions of impartial reasoning. The idea is to structure the discussion so that our theorizing about ethical matters will be informed by facts of individual cognitive capacities and dispositions under conditions dictated and controlled by the ideal theoretical structures. These data then replace the armchair conjectures that have often been used traditionally.

3. The complex intertwining of our definitions, knowledge claims, and theories, even about everyday concepts such as time, is illustrated by Hawking's (1988) interesting but controversial discussion.

a building erected on piles. The piles are driven down from above into the swamp, but not down to any natural or "given" base; and when we cease our attempts to drive our piles into a deeper layer, it is not because we have reached firm ground. We simply stop when we are satisfied that they are firm enough to carry the structure, at least for the time being.

Popper virtually stood common sense on its head by asserting that scientific laws can be tested but their truth cannot be known. Science and scientific progress, he argued, depend on a method that permits—indeed is committed to finding—falsification.[4] He concluded that our theories do not guarantee us positive theoretical knowledge. They give us tentative knowledge by allowing us to test propositions and ultimately point out what is not. The towering edifice of the contemporary natural sciences has emerged (almost literally) from the swamp, resting on the seemingly nihilistic principle of falsifiability. At the same time we often hear woeful comparisons between progress in science and the lack of progress in ethical knowledge. Popper's insights regarding science might serve as a guide to what standards are considered reasonable for knowledge claims in ethics.

Traditionally, many attempts to deal with ethical matters have searched for rock bottom. This has been the case since the ancients, for whom ethics and morals were tied to the gods, the priesthood, and the necessary. But to claim that science makes progress because the subject matter is open to testing and interpersonal verification/falsification while knowledge claims about ethical matters need "higher standards" involves chutzpa[5] of a high order. Nor is it surprising that moral philosophers have failed to embrace empirical methods. After all, for

4. In the years since this argument was put forth, a large number of comments have been made about this epistemological position. It has come under considerable fire but has also stood its ground quite well. The reader may wish to examine Maxwell (1972), Lakatos (1970), Jeffrey (1975), Miller (1975), and (an application of Miller) Abel and Oppenheimer (1982).

5. A Yiddish word imperfectly translated by the Greek *hubris* but better illustrated by the traditional story of the son who killed his mother and father and then threw himself on the mercy of the court on the grounds that he was an orphan.

many philosophers, ethical questions are shockingly beyond the empirical. Immanuel Kant [1785] (1959), for example, believed that insight into ethics required knowledge of necessary truths.[6] Other philosophers, glancing longingly at the greener grass on science's side of the fence, have commented on the lack of connection between arguments about values and science.[7]

Some philosophers (for example, deontologists), believing that ethical knowledge consists of necessary truths, try to demonstrate the necessity of their ethical view of the world. For them, anyone intellectually capable of following the twists and turns of their logical arguments, and wise enough to accept their premises as true, can discover the nature of ethical truth. Of course, the long-standing and continuing controversy among moral philosophers about the appropriate premises should serve as a warning that this approach is not likely to bear the fruit of cumulative knowledge. As Ernest Nagel (1961, pp. 53–54) has argued, the idea that scientific laws are necessarily true is antithetical to progressive improvement of those laws. After all, if a law is necessary, its denial would be a contradiction. As Nagel notes, this is not the way to proceed toward cumulative knowledge about empirical matters. His argument has obvious implications for other types of knowledge.

In mathematics there is little controversy regarding the relative quality of one axiom set over another. Indeed, one reason for the progress in mathematics is clear: there is a dual agreement. First, researchers agree on the desirability of discovering where different axiom sets lead, and, second, they agree to ac-

---

6. Köhler [1939] (1966) discusses this claim (pp. 43–45). Edel (1963, p. 19) also refers to this tendency and the role of Kant in the tradition of searching for necessary truths.

7. See, for example, Caws (1967). He was rather typical in his attempt to argue for the possibility of progress in the field of ethics by adopting the methods of science. But he refused to take the plunge. Drawing a parallel between observation statements in science (these are often argued to be a relatively important element in testing) and ethical intuition in ethics (p. 55 et seq.), he never once argued that we should or even could measure ethical intuition. The quote by Williams at the opening of Part 1 of this book is in the same spirit.

cept each axiom system on a par with every other as long as it is fruitful.[8] Compare this process to the typical activity in ethics. There, each philosopher extols the virtues of a particular set of axioms and tries to use it to discover the real nature of the good. In ethics, the schools of thought do battle with one another. As a result, necessary truths in ethics do not reflect the peculiar consensus among the well-trained that they do in other fields such as logic and mathematics.[9] If ethics were merely the study of alternative ethical systems, as mathematics is the study of alternative axiom systems, then perhaps we would look for many ethical theories and not the most accurate or correct ethical truths. But such an approach is clearly not what moral philosophers have in mind.

What does this discussion of ethical and scientific inquiry have to do with questions of distributive justice? The link lies in the prescriptions about methods. The typical moral philosopher is not found in the laboratory, while the natural scientist is. The differential progress in the natural sciences and in ethics may well stem from their differences in methods. And these methodological differences reflect the denial of the empirical in the study of ethical theory.

The major implication of the differential progress made with these different methods of inquiry is not difficult to sketch. Our methods reflect the basic notion that we are looking for theories that might be false and that are empirically testable. Our substantive concern—the nature of distributive justice understood as fairness—leads us to be concerned with empirical aspects of how people (from an impartial point of view) reason about moral matters and, as groups, make collective decisions about social justice. This act of actual human reasoning

8. It should be obvious from the fields of logic and mathematics that knowledge about necessary truths can be accumulated very powerfully with this method.

9. Of course, one might argue that the analogy with mathematical truths (rather than linguistic truths) is mistaken. Then the issue becomes what are the correct formal aspects of moral reasoning (cf. Raz 1978, especially the essays by Chisolm and Von Wright).

about ethical matters under carefully controlled and structured conditions has not been sufficiently investigated. It is not well understood by philosophers, social scientists, and social activists who build most heavily on its presumed nature. By structuring experimental conditions, we wed to the traditional theoretical approach an empirical one that informs us as normative theorists. In fact, our data indicate that some of the disputes among philosophers and social scientists may be moot or at least not finely to the point.

In presenting this methodology and our results, we have to evoke skepticism and a desire to test further. We will succeed when some readers are motivated to probe our methodological weaknesses, pursue the subject further, correct the findings, and drive the piles deeper.

IMPERFECTIONS IN THE EXPERIMENTAL DESIGN

Let us catalogue the potential problems with our experiments by indicating how they fall short of the ideal case. We have argued that any principle of distributive justice consistently affirmed under ideal conditions of impartial reasoning has a claim as a just principle. If one principle were always chosen by any set of human beings under any or all such conditions it would have an unassailable claim.

Our experiments fall short of the ideal in at least two obvious ways. First, although they attempt to approximate ideal conditions, they are but distant approximations along a number of dimensions. Second, our subject pool does not adequately sample humanity. The details of these shortcomings need to be described to help define the limitations to our findings and the challenges for future work.

Representativeness

The simplest problem is the representativeness of our subjects. As in many experiments in the behavioral sciences, our subject pool consisted of students at public universities. Not in Canada, the United States, or Poland are university students representative of the population. Most clearly, students tend to be about the same age: late teens and early twenties. Furthermore, although all classes are represented to some degree, children of upper- and upper-middle-class families are overrepresented in universities. Given their backgrounds, life experiences, and future prospects (they have all at least made it through admission into college), we should be concerned that their expectations in life are not representative of those of the population as a whole. And they may well project these expectations into their choice of principle. In particular, not expecting to be "on the bottom" in the real world might bias their supposedly impartial decision process.

Although it cannot be ruled out, there is some evidence from the experiments to cause us to discount that potential bias. In our questionnaire, students were asked to indicate acceptable income levels for themselves at various future points in their lives. Had aspirations in the real world intruded on their choices, one would have expected these aspirations to have significant predictive power regarding preferences for principles. They did not. Measures of political ideology and party affiliation also failed to predict preferences of principles significantly. The preference for the floor-constraint principle was evident across all the subgroups.

However, background considerations did affect the level of the floor that the groups set. The height of the safety net was determined partially by the subjects' underlying attitudes regarding income distribution. Subjects' attitudes toward the role of government as an insurer of welfare and as an arbiter of distributive claims were related to the groups' setting of floor incomes.

Rather than being a weakness in the experimental design, we view this as a necessary component of the choice of the groups in the experiments. Setting a floor income requires balancing values of need and entitlement while preserving incentives for work and productivity. So a just floor constraint for a society with a mean annual income of $20,000 per capita will differ from that for a society with $300 per capita. Indeed, the floor must take into account the socially possible. Individuals' perceptions of the relationships both between need and entitlement and between production and incentives will differ. These complex tradeoffs require personal knowledge of the relationships and personal values about them. In experiments, the subjects bring the values and knowledge and apply them. Thus the level of the floor chosen in experiments must reflect, in part, the subjects' weightings of the competing ethical imperatives of need and entitlement and their concerns and beliefs regarding incentives. It is therefore neither surprising nor problematic that different samples of subjects make differing tradeoffs among the competing values. What is surprising is that even with diverse values subjects can agree that a floor must be set and can agree to such a floor.[10]

The challenges opened by our limited sample of subjects are clear. Would a sample of working poor or welfare recipients or successful entrepreneurs reach similar conclusions?[11] Would people at different stages in life choose differently? Does the decision turn finely on the intellectual sophistication and reasoning power of the subjects? Our subjects were mainly representative of Western Judeo-Christian populations. Would the results hold up in Eastern cultures, in aboriginal cultures?[12] We cannot claim that they do, although we have strong hunches that the factors generating the results are general enough to stand up to wider sampling. One must be careful in using any set of observations to generalize to a whole society or to many

10. Of course, another implication flows. Say one wished to use this sort of experiment to ascertain a principle of distributive justice for a particular society. Because the subject pool's characteristics help set the level of the floor, it would be important that the subject pool be representative of that society.

11. Two imperfect replications of the basic experiments with retired businessmen in Winnipeg led to support for the floor-constraint principle. Although the basic experimental handbook was used, conditions did not allow for a full and carefully controlled experiment.

12. The work by Bond and Park (1991) using South Korean and American students was sufficiently different to preclude its consideration as a replication of our experiments. See footnote 22.

societies.[13] The only way to tell whether the results are generalizable is to expand the experimental base.[14]

Divergence from the Ideal Conditions of Impartial Reasoning

Our experiments diverge from the ideal conditions of impartial reasoning in a number of ways. In particular, three of these divergences pose real threats to the validity of the results. These threats come from three aspects of the experimental setup: group size, the levels of stakes in the experiments, and the duration of the experiments.

All the experiments were run with five-person groups. The size of the decision-making group might make a difference. The individuals were not well known to each other (to rule out antecedent personal attachments), but the groups were small enough to allow for personal interaction. It might be that in such small groups an unusual degree of solidarity and trust can build up. Conceivably this effect would lead to a choice that a larger group might not make. Indeed, one group's discussion explicitly touched on that point (see Chapter 7).

The dispute about the effect of group size on individuals' incentives to contribute to group efforts is long-standing. A rule that redistributes income earned by individual effort has an element of a social dilemma in it: a guaranteed floor raises the moral hazard that those who are low producers may slack off and free ride on the efforts of others. Mancur Olson (1965) argued that individuals in small groups were much more likely than those in large ones to make voluntary contributions to group efforts. That contention was disputed by us (Frohlich and Oppenheimer 1971). Numerous experiments have been done on social dilemmas since that time, and the issue is still not

13. The need for caution in generalizing was emphasized with almost hysterical force by a high government official in Poland in 1988. Upon hearing a presentation of our results dealing with participation and productivity (and facing demands by workers for increased participation in decision making), he forcefully listed possible threats to the external validity of the results.

14. Experiments to test the reactions of nonstudents are in the preliminary stages in Australia.

resolved (see Isaac, Walker, and Williams 1990). But clearly some scale effects are more than possible. For example, in small groups working at some tasks, information costs are lower and cost-benefit calculations more viable than in larger groups. To check these possibilities experiments would have to be performed with groups of differing sizes.

Group size might also affect the ability of a group to reach unanimity. Whenever groups of five were allowed to continue their discussions until they either reached an impasse or reached consensus, they were able to agree on a principle. Larger groups might well have difficulties in achieving that level of agreement. To test for a scale effect it would be necessary to extend the time frame and find a mechanism whereby all participants could make their positions clear and engage in give and take. In very large groups, meeting those requirements would be difficult. But, again, the theoretical possibility is open to experimental test.

The size of the subject's stake in the decisions is another variable that was held relatively constant in our experiments. Subjects might choose differently and behave differently if the stakes were much higher than $40 for a few hours "work," especially if, as Rawls would have it, they were deciding their whole life chances and those of all society for all time to come.[15] But, given the tone of the discussions (most of them framed as a choice of rules for society), we doubt that the results of such experiments would be very different. Subjects seemed seriously intent on discussing need, entitlement, and incentives, and the appropriate tradeoffs among them. The floor-constraint principle furnishes the vehicle for the tradeoffs, and therein lies its attraction. The results do not seem sensitive to scale-of-payoff effects.

The stakes were restricted not only in size but in duration.

15. Subjects might well give prior consent to the making of decisions under what they know to be hypothetical conditions. They might be induced to participate in experiments under hypnosis in which they are led to believe that the stakes are indeed life chances. This would increase our ability to test otherwise unrealizable conditions.

Our typical experiment lasted between one and two hours. That's hardly a lifetime. It is not clear whether the subjects' enthusiasm for the redistributions would have persevered over longer periods. The experiments tested only productivity as a function of effort and contained no investment component. Perhaps long-term investment behavior could change as a function of experience with the redistribution. Again, the only way to tell is to run extended experiments and to see whether the effects of choosing from an impartial point of view wear off as subjects experience the consequences not three times but many. The cumulative impact of redistribution might well be different over a longer time period.

The size of the groups, the size of the stakes, and the restricted length of the experiments all fall far from the ideal. Evidence gleaned from the conversations may give us some insight into how well the experimental conditions evoked the desired state. The reading of the transcripts is somewhat but not unequivocally reassuring. The discussions as a set display a certain ambiguity regarding the verisimilitude of subjects' deliberations. A few groups discussed the payoffs predominantly as immediate dollar amounts available to them. Most groups discussed the payoffs in the context of society and annual incomes, but many of those had discussions that moved in and out of the individual/societal modes.

SUBJECT 1: But are we talking about ourselves going to get that money or are we talking about a society? [I think] . . . we're deciding in this experiment . . . for . . . us. . . . You know, they can do the generalizations afterward.

SUBJECT 2: You see we're like a little model of the whole economy right now. (*Transcripts*, p. 287)

What's best for society, we'd better figure, is best for us. (*Transcripts*, p. 328)

These ambiguities underscore the need for replication and refinements of the experiments. But it is not clear that one could ever successfully remove the conflict between the actual dollar payoffs and their symbolic significance. It may be an inherent problem with the experimental method.

The experimental design and specific wording of the instruments are another possible threat to the validity of the results. Experiments with human beings are tricky and subtle affairs. Experimenters may sometimes, quite unwittingly, insert clues in the wording of their instructions that subjects pick up on. There is no sure way of protecting against such experimental biases, although a double-blind experimental design would have helped. In constructing the instruments we attempted to be impartial in presenting the four principles, but (given our own arguments in the Introduction about the difficulties of achieving that objective) we certainly cannot guarantee we succeeded. When the experiments were first designed, however, we had no idea whether subjects could reach agreement and, if so, what that agreement might be. We informally concluded that subjects would probably concoct their own principle, which would be a combination of a floor and range constraint. The dominance of the floor-constraint principle became apparent only after the full-scale experiments began. Because we had not anticipated that result (or favored it *ex ante*), it would have been difficult to bias the instrument consciously in that direction.

The problem of possible experimenter bias exists not only in the wording of the instrument but also in the protocol of the experiments: the specific series of activities through which the subjects were led. In the choice experiments, the subjects chose principles and were randomly assigned to income classes to experience the consequences of their choices. The luck of the draw placed some high up, while others fared poorly. The intent was to have subjects experience the principles in action after impartiality was removed, but we cannot be sure exactly what they may have learned from those experiences. The same is true of their discussions, their group choices, and their subsequent production. Would they have chosen (acted) differently if they had worked first, perhaps at some unrelated task? Did the order in which we organized the activities matter? We do not know. But these empirical questions can be addressed in future work.

Other aspects of the design are possibly problematic as well. It would have been better to have discussion in the experiments where we imposed the principle. By covarying the two conditions (discussion and choice) we were unable to segregate the effects of discussion from the effects of choice. Thus, it is impossible for us to tell whether the increased productivity by recipients of transfers stems from participation in the democratic decision process or from the discussion.[16] Furthermore, we cannot tell whether the observed effects were due to the discussion of redistributive principles or would have been generated by any generic discussion process.[17] However, the tone of the discussions would indicate that the substance of the discussion had a lot to do with the outcomes in the experiments.[18] In addition, in the production experiments, taxes were assessed and withheld. Subjects received their net wages at each stage of the experiment along with a report of their gross earnings. Had they received their gross wages and then been taxed, their reactions might have been different.[19]

We can also criticize our operationalization of the principles. We illustrated the principles in the first part of the experiments by linking different income distributions to different prin-

16. Recall that the different effect on productivity of the transfer recipients between discussion/choice and nondiscussion/nonchoice groups did not take place immediately. Rather, it surfaced only after the first round of production. This result hints that it is the combination of economic experience and participation in choosing the rule that affects the performance. Had discussion/choice been the only factor, differences in productivity presumably would have appeared immediately.

17. Dawes, McTavish, and Shaklee (1977) have produced evidence, however, that only relevant discussion increases cooperative behavior in social-dilemma situations.

18. Anyone interested in doing analyses of the transcripts can receive them, on computer disks or paper, for the price of duplication, handling, and mailing.

19. Although this procedure may be thought of as a flaw, it is consistent with practices in most industrialized countries, where income taxes are withheld at source.

ciples. The principle of maximum income was always associated with the income with the lowest floor. That operationalization was based on the notion that the less redistribution
required to raise the floor the more economic incentive would
remain to lift the overall productivity in the society. The difference principle, by contrast and by the same reasoning, had the
highest floor and the lowest average. The two other principles
(floor constraint and range constraint) had intermediate-level
floors and intermediate-level averages because they required
more redistribution than maximum income and less than the
different principle. Table 29 can serve as an example; it presents
the first situation in which subjects chose a principle. A subject's choice of a principle identified a single distribution as the
most just, and she or he was randomly assigned to one of the
classes within that distribution and paid off accordingly.

It was presumed that subjects would learn some of the implied tradeoffs in the principles via their choices and experiences. In the high-stakes experiments, the sample situations
were changed to make the floors lower and the ceilings higher
in order to emphasize the differences among the principles and
to increase the stakes. This change appears not to have affected
behavior significantly.

It should be emphasized that in the experiments in which
subjects worked to earn income they did not make sample
choices prior to working. Thus in those experiments there was
less experimenter definition of the principles via exemplary
distributions. Yet, in these experiments, when subjects played
a bigger role in defining the principles, their choices were similar to those made under the experimenter-defined protocol.

Another possible imperfection in the experimental design
was the explicit inclusion of only four principles. As noted at
the outset, these were chosen from Rawls's agenda (1971) and
covered all the principles he would have considered.[20] We went
to pains to mention, at each experimental phase, that subjects

20. This classification assumes that the group size is fixed so that maximizing total utility and maximizing average utility are the same.

Table 29. Illustration of Operationalization of Principles

Income Class	Income Distributions			
	1	*2*	*3*	*4*
High	$28,000	$35,000	$30,000	$25,000
Medium high	25,000	30,000	29,000	22,000
Medium	20,000	25,000	28,000	19,000
Medium low	15,000	15,000	27,000	16,000
Low	12,000	10,000	6,000	13,000
Average income	20,000	23,500	26,000	19,000
Floor or low income	12,000	10,000	6,000	13,000
Range	16,000	25,000	24,000	12,000

Note: If the principle was maximum income, distribution 3 was chosen; if it was the difference principle, distribution 4 was selected. Setting a floor constraint of between $10,000 and $12,999 made distribution 2 the choice, while setting a range constraint below $16,000 made distribution 4 the choice.

could introduce principles of their own devising; and in a few cases groups concocted mixed principles. So the agenda was not completely closed, and any unforeseen candidates for principles of distributive justice had a chance to emerge.[21]

Finally, random effects impinge on our experiments as they do on any. We have already mentioned one: the particular trajectory of discussions in some groups because of a single dominant individual. Only replication in large numbers can give us confidence that what appears to be a general trend is not just a statistical artifact. But here, again, the experimental methodology makes it possible to do the tests.

IMPLICATIONS

We have shown experimental methods to be useful in the study of distributive justice in particular and potentially for ethics in general. Our experimental results are preliminary and are open to criticism. But the results appear robust. If subsequent research confirms the findings, there are lessons to be learned.

What can we carry away from this long voyage through our experimental laboratory? To highlight the implications from the study we cluster them to parallel the issues that motivated the research. Viewed that way, the implications fall into three major categories: for the theory of distributive justice, for the methodology of ethical inquiry, and for social policy.

Implications for the Theory of Distributive Justice

Perhaps the single most striking and important finding is the apparent universality, strength, and robustness of a consensus-building "decision device." The ideal conditions of impartial reasoning, as operationalized in the laboratory, were extraordinarily successful in generating consensual decisions about distributive justice. The thinness of the veil behind which subjects reasoned and the simplicity of the operationalization are

21. In designing the original experiments we expected that subjects would construct their own principles, and we viewed the list as a guide only.

both testimony to the robustness and general applicability of the philosophical concept. Because considerable skepticism has often been expressed regarding the realizability of mechanisms to generate impartiality, this finding is central.

Equally surprising was the consistency of the group choices. Relatively weak conditions generated an almost determinate result (setting an income floor). Although consensus on that particular principle was generally unanticipated, many scholars had argued that one could generate a determinate choice. With the benefit of hindsight, determinate choice appears quite justifiable. After all, it has been a fundamental article of faith of many philosophers that impartial reasoning should yield a determinate result. Many others dealing with fairness in a common-sense fashion have also believed that people could identify and agree on what is truly fair. It was a much stronger, and perhaps daring, conjecture of game theorists and Rawlsian philosophers to argue that a particular mechanism (a veil of ignorance) could, in the ideal, yield a definitive outcome.

Although their theories predicted consensus on a principle, they did not agree among themselves about *which* principle would emerge. Harsanyi argued for maximizing utility and Rawls for maximizing the primary goods of the worst-off. Both of their conjectures proved wrong. But there was a consensus. As in many philosophical debates, the result appears to have been somewhere in the middle. And the theorists who predicted the outcome, Howe and Roemer (1981), seem to have reached the right conclusion but for the wrong reason. There does not appear to be a relationship between the individuals' attitudes toward risk aversion and their desire to establish a social safety net. The desire to find a compromise between incentives and security, as it unfolds in the discussions leading to a setting of a floor, appears not to rest on attitudes about risk. Rather, rejection of competing principles and setting a floor seem predicated on a desire to balance claims of entitlements and needs, while preserving incentives for productivity. The floor-constraint principle provides the flexibility to permit these tradeoffs in different degrees.

Thus the substance of the findings is quite interesting: consensus appears to be universally feasible and there is little variance in the result as long as the structure of the choice environment conforms to the conditions specified theoretically.[22] It appears that there may be sufficient consistency in human nature to generate consensus on questions of distributive justice.

The experimental mechanism uncovers support for letting people keep what they earn, without a ceiling, after providing for a floor, or safety net. This agreement appears basic in our data: it is not reducible to other factors that we measured. It emerges, without prompting, in an environment in which self-interest cannot be fully identified. Not only is it a consensual choice by the groups, but the rankings of all of the principles by the individuals in all locations showed strong similarities. Thus, it does not appear that culture—even value differences about the legitimacy and desirability of redistribution—matters when it comes to generating agreement about a principle for redistribution. Moreover, differences in group choices that do emerge do not reflect cultural patterns. The floor constraint appears to have generalizable appeal.

The considerable agreement on the particular rule does not spill over into agreement on a specific level for the social safety net or floor. Here cultural variables have great effect. Indeed, one could imagine that the level of the floor that is set is almost a strict function of the average, or perhaps the median, of value positions of the individuals who are making the decisions.

Rawls anticipated an effect like this. One of his major objections to mixed or intuitionistic principles was that it would be impossible to get unanimity about the full definition of the principle. The result of maximum income is quite clear, as is that of maximizing the floor. But if one talks about a floor con-

---

22. An interesting study that began as a replication of our experiments was conducted in Korea and the United States by Bond and Park (1991). In those experiments the conditions of choice were modified somewhat. The changes in the conditions made the structure of the distributions in question zero sum. Because there was no incentive to produce more, the experiments led to choices that either predominantly maximized the floor or specified range constraints. But because neither the real world nor the world envisioned by most theorists is zero sum in nature, these results are not directly germane to our findings.

straint, one is immediately led to ask: "At what level should one set the floor?" Rawls could not imagine the particular information or values of representative individuals that would lead to a consensus on the specific level for the floor. Even if the mixed principle were popular, Rawls could not envision how participants behind a hypothesized veil of ignorance could or would come to an agreement regarding the level of the constraints.[23]

In reality, Rawls's conjecture was partially right: individuals disagree on the proper level of the floor; no intergroup consistency across experiments emerges.[24] But (and this is a crucial *but* for theorists such as Rawls) groups of real individuals under conditions approximating the ideal conditions of impartial reasoning do generally reach consensus regarding the level of the floor constraint. They do it through discussion and political compromise in a dynamic, evolving process. Their decisions show central tendencies, but there is some cultural variation.

This variation might be thought to generate an assault on the universal acceptability of any mixed principle. And yet again, in retrospect, with the benefit of the data from the experiments, we can see why some context should enter into a determination of what is fair. Consider a thought experiment of a sort Rawls did not anticipate. Imagine running our basic experiment in a reasonably well off medieval European village. It would be ludicrous to imagine that any such group would hit on a floor constraint of anything approaching the equivalent of $10,000 per annum. Such a village might well qualify as an

23. In attempting to replicate our experiments in Korea, Bond and his partner expressed the same concern. In a personal communication to us, Bond worried that subjects would not be able to agree on a level for the floor. To make the problem easier for them they changed the income distributions so that the average income for all distributions was the same. This procedure had the effect of removing many of the incentives for higher productivity and changing the nature of the choices.

24. It probably is worth pointing out that within a broad cultural group, such as is found in North America, we find something close to a normal distribution of such constraints. Including Poland, however, creates a bimodal, skewed distribution. One would expect this result when a sample is taken from two different populations.

economy of moderate scarcity as Rawls required. Yet their notion of what would be a fair support level for a floor constraint would necessarily be tied to a consideration of what was possible in their own context. Moreover, it would be tied to their mental pictures of what all parties in the situations would get in the end. We could expect to be able to generalize the nature of the fairest rule found by our groups to the medieval case, but we could not be expected to translate the dollar value directly. Perhaps the proper measure of the height of the safety net is an adequate minimum earned income in the society.[25]

Rawls was right, intuitionistic principles are not rigid enough to yield absolute agreement. They involve some relativism and flexibility. Filling in the information necessary to render them operational in a given context requires the provision of contextually dependent information. The context has to be literally fleshed out. Subjects in an appropriately structured experimental situation do that.

And when subjects do reach agreement, the experimental evidence also speaks to the main criticism of theories of distributive justice based on patterns of distribution. Champions of entitlements argue that any redistributive principle might well be subject to eroding support after the veil is lifted. People, the argument goes, will begin to feel the negative consequences of the taxation that is required to support the weak and will feel hard done by. Our evidence says that this criticism is dubious. Strong support continues for the group choice regarding distributive justice after subjects experience their role in the scheme of things. Howe and Roemer, who argued for this result if a redistributive principle were to set a floor and then permit maximization of returns, appear correct.

But the stability does not appear to come from Howe and Roemer's notion that the floor-constraint principle incorporates different senses of risk aversion. The source of the stabil-

---

25. Some works, and some social policies, have been written with this measure in mind. See Lebergott (1976, pp. 53–69).

ity seems to be far less individualistic; it seems rather to be the result of the emergence of the social acceptance and bonding engendered in the discussion and choice. And the support is strengthened as a function of experience with the rule for those who participated in framing it from an impartial point of view.

But the conjectured erosion of psychological support for the principle is not the only threat to the continued viability of a principle agreed on. Economists, even some of those most sensitive to issues of distributive justice and most ideologically oriented toward these findings, have often exaggerated the difficulty of achieving distributive justice while preserving continued productivity. So, for example, Sen has written (1973, p. 94): "It would be in the interest of each person to pretend to be less productive than he is and then to take things easy. By producing less oneself one reduces total output by a relatively small amount, and under equality[26] the impact on one's net income is minute."

Thus Sen construes production as a social or prisoners' dilemma game (p. 97). As is now widely known, there are two solutions to such dilemmas: the Nash equilibrium and the core. It has often been asserted incorrectly that the two solutions reflect two different orientations: individual (Nash) and collective (core). But the core is a stable solution concept precisely because it reflects the individual's incentives. It gains stability because the individual cannot guarantee himself or herself more by changing strategic choices. Indeed, there have been innumerable experiments of prisoners' dilemma games that show that many circumstances generate outcomes in the core. Still, Sen and others tend to emphasize the rejectability of the collective solution. As Sen (pp. 97–98) put it: "Since a collective contract with provision for enforcement may be extremely difficult to devise for labour efforts, the lesson to be drawn here has to be different. Work supervision to ensure adherence to a 'sincere effort' contract involves many problems,

26. Or, we would argue, under any similar, relatively egalitarian concept.

and this is precisely where an incentive system of wages has an advantage."[27]

Our evidence casts doubt on the generality of this position. If individuals, using an impartial procedure, participate and then agree on a fair rule for redistribution, they generate a commitment to the principle. At least in small groups this outcome resolves some of the feared conflicts between redistribution and incentives to produce. In the experiments there are no measurable drops in the efforts of those who stand to gain by free-riding in the social dilemma. Those below the floor could take it easy in their task and still take home the same amount. They don't! After they participate in the decision they increase their productivity significantly. The low producers are the individuals who make the extra effort. Perhaps this extra effort reflects their owning of the contract. Their counterparts who do not participate in choosing their fates show no such cooperative outlook. They decrease their effort and productivity. When workers do not have a say in the rules that govern their rewards, the critics may have a case.

The implications are considerable. This evidence, garnered in our labs, flies, in part, against some of the austere prognoses of modern social theory. As Sen (1990, p. 54) puts it:

> In many economic and social theories today, human beings are seen as strict maximizers of a narrowly defined self-interest, and given that relentless compulsion, pessimism about social rearrangements to reduce inequality will indeed be justified. But not only is that "model" of human beings depressing and dreary, there is very little evidence that it is a good representation of reality. People are influenced not only by the perception of their own interests, but also, as Albert Hirschman puts it, by their passions. Indeed, among the things that seem to move people, whether in Prague or Paris or Warsaw or Beijing or Little Rock or Johannesburg, are concern for others and regard for ideas.

27. Sen then turns to the notion that culture would be the major determinant so as to change a prisoners' dilemma game into an "assurance game" (p. 98). But this is not what we find. Our results do not appear to be a question of culture or even of expectation.

To repeat, there are threats to the generalizability of this result. Our economic tasks were simple; there was no serious role differentiation in our economy; there was no investment over time; the groups were small; and the experiments lasted only a limited time. But in this simplified world of the laboratory we got a result that has been found in other, more complex, situations. The experience of Israeli kibbutzim and cooperative enterprises in Northern Europe, North America, and elsewhere has demonstrated that success is possible, but possibly short-lived.[28]

Implications for the Methodology of Ethical Inquiry

We begin with one tentative existence claim: at least one device exists for discovering some content of a fair rule of distributive justice. Approximating the ideal conditions of impartial reasoning in a laboratory can yield consensus on what is fair. That finding applies to one family of ethical problems. There are other families of ethical problems that we have not addressed here. But there are also possibilities for further generalizations and findings. The lessons we have begun to learn may be far richer and broader than they first appear. The same experimental device for inducing impartial reasoning might well be applicable to other families of problems (for example, to a wider class of prisoners' dilemma games).[29]

The device we have employed also shows us that it is difficult to predict, a priori, the domains over which consistent agreement is possible from an impartial point of view. We found virtual unanimity on the fairest principle but not the same degree of unanimity on a specific floor. Which compo-

28. After all, many of these cooperatives deteriorate once their constitutions ossify and new members enter who did not participate in the constitutional debates.

29. Frohlich (1991) has explicitly applied the theoretical veil of ignorance to the classic two-person prisoners' dilemma to show how the cooperative solution would be chosen from an impartial point of view. The analysis presents arguments that help explain the prevalence of observed cooperative behavior in laboratory tests of play in the game. A group of undergraduates at the University of Maryland ran experiments on a subset of cases conforming to this hypothesis and found results that were highly significant. (See Canova et al. 1990.)

nents of an ethical principle can generate unanimity and which cannot may not yet be predictable. That information may have to be "discovered" by careful design of experiments. The result may well be insight into rules that allow for increasingly accurate future predictions in other domains, or it may be a realization that there is no substitute for continuing empirical inquiry.

One of the major strengths of the experimental approach is its capacity to introduce real individual values. We, with the help of our "naive" subjects, have concluded that the question of distributive justice involves competing claims of entitlements, need, and the desirability of preserving incentives. If an ethically problematic situation involves a conflict between competing values, then the strength and weight of those values have to be taken into consideration in the determination of what is fair. The experimental method provides that device. It brings real representative individuals into the arena, bearing their own values, which can be applied from an impartial point of view. If one finds, with a broad sampling of humanity, that they can reach consensus, it is strong presumptive evidence for the just content of their decision. By contrast, one might find that in applying the device to similar problems, with different samples of humanity, different principles gain support. In those cases, justice might be viewed as contingent. One's attention might be drawn to the differences in underlying values that yield the different results.

We have made one existence claim: there is one "powerful" device for discovering the content of an ethical principle. It is not wild to conjecture that there probably exist other devices (numerous, or at least a few) for discovering the content of ethical principles. This possibility would seem to be a reason, by itself, to run empirical experiments to discover the nature of such devices. They could be used to identify the content, and the variation in content, that might exist in some of the categories of ethical decisions about which we have conjectured for millennia. We are led to argue for the broad use of empirical tools in examining such areas of ethical inquiry as fiduciary relations, promise keeping, and possibly others.

Implications for Social Policy

Under conditions of impartiality, the floor-constraint principle was the overwhelming choice as a substantive principle of distributive justice. It also has stability properties. Given these findings, an acceptable income-support program for those in need should be a real political possibility. Indeed, income-support programs provided in Western democracies appear to be founded on the floor-constraint principle. These programs supposedly define a safety net to catch the unfortunate. Yet across many jurisdictions one sees variations in abject poverty: groups and classes of individuals who live below what surely must be an acceptably fair floor. What we find is that social support programs are often among the most contentious political issues in Western democracies. They are a source of constant concern, legislative infighting, and tinkering. How can that dissentious scene be squared with the wide consensus we found about the floor-constraint principle? What mechanisms block the implementation of a policy that could have broad-based support?

We believe there are four major obstacles to the adequate implementation of social support programs with a fair and meaningful floor constraint. All those obstacles are manifest in differences between our experimental environment and that found in full-scale democratic societies. In society as opposed to our experiments: (1) social support policies are not agreed on under conditions of impartial reasoning; (2) people do not actively and meaningfully participate in the debate on the appropriate support programs; (3) people do not know what the real level of need is among those requiring support or about the actual benefits received; (4) people do not have adequate information about the efforts being made by those who rely on support programs. All these factors are exacerbated by the fact that in mass society the size of the population poses major impediments to meaningful participation and the dissemination of information. To see how these factors affect the difficulty of getting consensus and implementing a support program, the factors can be looked at in detail.

The most obvious point is that political choices, even in democracies, are not made from an impartial point of view. Politicians and voting publics know who they are when they debate and vote on policies. Forming coalitions to establish or maintain parochial interests is a widely accepted attribute of the democratic process. Thus, only to the extent that there is some uncertainty about everyone's fate can one expect a demand for programs that establish floors. For good or ill, no one can be sure of what tomorrow may bring. As a result, social security programs are widespread. They are insurance against the contingencies that are revealed as we all proceed through the veil that shrouds our futures. But the future provides an imperfect veil, for we all have a reasonably good knowledge of our current assets, tastes, and roles in society. And if we cannot have certainty, we can at least make some estimates of the probabilities of future contingencies. Support programs, given human nature, reflect that imperfection in the operative veil and are likely to be imperfectly fair.

But the lack of impartiality is not the only aspect of real political decisions that makes the establishment and maintenance of fair support policies difficult. In our experiments, discussion and participation mattered. Within small groups, explicit discussion of what constitutes fairness establishes the need for, and legitimacy of, some sort of support program. But meaningful participation was also necessary to shape the future behavior of participants. It is not clear that such participation can be engineered in groups as large as a whole society or a region. Indeed, communes and kibbutzim perhaps mark the temporal and size dimensions of meaningful participatory incentives without extensive social engineering. To extend these parameters some good ideas would seem to be needed for forming participatory systems that could engender social identification for large groups.[30]

There are two major themes that pervade the arguments of

30. This observation should not be taken to mean that it would be impossible to develop such structures. For example, federated discussion groups, each of which would have to come to collective decisions, might be possible.

both politicians and citizens who attack income-support programs: (1) An income-support program will sap incentives among recipients and make them dependent and unproductive. (2) Income support will create a moral hazard and attract the "undeserving," the "welfare cheaters," which is unfair to all those who work and ultimately pay for the programs. Our results indicate that when those who ultimately are to be recipients of transfers participate actively in the decision, increasing dependence and sloth do not materialize. Quite the contrary. It would appear that recipients who actively participate in the decision recognize the entitlement claims of those who are paying for transfer payments and almost literally redouble their efforts to pull their own weight. By contrast, when recipients function under a (functionally identical) income-support system that has been imposed on them and in which they have had no substantial say, they produce less. Their efforts flag and their productivity declines. They appear to view the transfers they receive as their due, and they do not make efforts to become self-sustaining. Genuine participation and debate in determining the content of programs thus appear necessary to prevent the undermining of income-support programs.

Large-scale democracies contain a barrier for the application of our results. In them, having one's deeply felt concerns heard, debated (perhaps clarified and altered), and reflected in policy outcomes is a luxury reserved for the very few. Participation falls far short of the levels experienced in our groups. Indeed, there is a well-known propensity in democratic systems for political activity to decrease with decreasing socioeconomic status. Thus, there would appear to be a need for increased participation in the political process across all strata if stable support programs are to be established and maintained. And, of course, there are enormous barriers to the implementation, writ large, of the kind of process that we have set up in the laboratory. But our data point to the desirability of informed debate and participation. Without it the fears that income support cannot be easily sustained may be well founded.

Within our experimental groups, agreement on the floor-constraint principle transcends differences in ideology and partisanship. The same is true to a lesser extent regarding the level of the floor. What disagreement there is on the appropriate level of the floor appears to be subject to political compromise. Why then is it so difficult to get agreement on an appropriate floor in ongoing democracies? In addition to the factors noted, the relatively low levels of information in the population make such a consensus difficult. Citizens, for reasons that Anthony Downs (1957) articulated in his seminal book, simply do not have incentives to become well informed on issues of broad social policy.

Given low levels of information, political differences are bound to arise on the bases of different perceptions of the facts. One encounters many political conservatives and liberals who agree that some support programs are necessary. But their notions of acceptable floors are colored by different perceptions of what people at the bottom need in order to lead nondegrading lives. Most upper-middle- and upper-class individuals do not have a clear notion of the minimal income level needed to support a family. Nor do they appreciate what the poverty line means and what it is like to live beneath it. And they have little incentive or opportunity to find out. The stories that are most likely to catch their attention deal with the excesses of those living in poverty (on welfare) or of gross welfare cheaters. Thus a small number of spectacular cases can color the perceptions of the average taxpayer, who then has every incentive to support reductions in social support programs (that is, in lowering the floor). The continual flow of stories is likely to render any program involving real transfers contentious.[31]

Perceived lack of effort by those at the bottom can also un-

31. Of course contributory schemes such as Social Security in the United States and the Canada Pension in Canada are able to rise above this contentiousness much of the time. Because they are contributory, beneficiaries are seen as having entitlements that are not subject to charges of abuse. The force of this argument can be seen by noting the bases of the political attempts to change benefits in these programs. The argument is always made that some benefit is unfair or unfunded.

dermine support by those who must pay for transfers. This effect was observed directly (but informally) in one of our pilot production experiments. A very productive subject in the first round appeared to be aghast and incredulous at the fact that one of the five group members was unable to find and correct a single error in the text. The high producer was a major subsidizer of that very poor speller (or lazy worker). At the start of the second round, the high producer put down his pencil and did not try to correct errors in the text. It appeared that he was refusing to work to support the free-rider. Instead, he sat and stared at the low producer. After a minute or so, it became apparent that the low producer was reading the text and working very hard to try to find errors. The high producer, realizing that the other's poor performance was due not to lack of effort but simply to inferior ability, picked up his pencil and worked feverishly for the next two minutes.

The point of this anecdote is that in our experiments subjects were able to get information on one another's real effort and real incomes (from the experiments). When they had that information they were quite happy with a floor-constraint principle that sometimes redistributed significant amounts of income. There was universal agreement that those in genuine need had a legitimate claim. The values and behavior of those who bore the costs transcended the vulgar notions of rational and narrowly self-interested economic actors. In society, upper- and middle-class people have little appreciation for what those who are disadvantaged can do and are doing to help themselves. They have no real appreciation of the difficulty of finding remunerative employment when one is undereducated or handicapped in some way. When instances of flagrant free-riding are found and publicized, they tend to overshadow the many instances of genuine need and to undercut the legitimacy of those programs that have been implemented. This undermining can be furthered because politicians with well-off constituents have interests in biasing the information their constituents receive. They can make welfare an issue by bringing forward horror stories and can garner support on the basis of promises to reform the system (and, of course, to decrease the tax burden).

In our experiments, when subjects do not participate in choosing their redistributional scheme, a measure of free-riding is found among those at the bottom. On average, subjects fail to gain confidence in their support of the floor-contraint principle. High earners who have not actively wrestled with the need for supports are not as committed to the programs and are more skeptical than those who have actively debated the matter and chosen their principle. Recipients who have not participated may treat the transfers they receive as a right and may not increase their efforts in order to unburden their fellows. In large-scale democracies, the experiences of taxpayers and recipients are more likely to reflect those of subjects who did not actively debate and choose their principle. As a result, these effects of free-riding and skepticism may cumulate over time, and in a nonparticipatory democracy one might expect some erosion of support for programs.

Even were a just principle to be agreed on, there would be impediments to implementing it in a fair fashion. The simple model of fairness that motivated Rawls—the cake-cutting example with two persons—is itself imperfect in implementation. True the cutter has every incentive to be as fair as possible and to divide the cake into two even pieces. The cutter knows that if one piece is bigger the chooser will take it. But the cutter is only human, and perfect division is not usually attainable. So most people offered a choice of cutter or chooser will choose to choose. They implicitly know about the difficulty of cutting fairly. That problem is found writ large in social programs. As we have seen, the floor-constraint principle incorporates competing claims of need, entitlements, and incentives. The mix must be a careful blend of the three. In large-scale societies it is difficult for both legislators and citizens to get the information necessary to make those tradeoffs and to convince themselves of their fairness.

It appears that agreement among a small group in the laboratory may be stable. The hope offered by our results is that there is an underlying implicit consensus that can form the basis for fair social policies. If such policies are to succeed in society, they must continue to be acceptable and cannot undermine productivity. But as we have argued, on a large scale a number of political problems tied to the costs of information and participation are likely to arise. These practical problems call out for solutions. Increased communication and meaningful participation in the political process may be required for the continued acceptability of reasonable support programs. Nor is such a prospect totally unreasonable.

A practical—though still relatively small-scale—example of the possible efficacy of involving workers in decisions is demonstrated by the evidence emerging from the industrial relations literature. Profit-sharing schemes, participation in workplace quality-of-life issues, the use of quality circles, and a general openness of management to the suggestions from the shop floor are all beginning to show promise of increasing worker productivity. The necessity of participation in such schemes is reflected in this quote (Kanter 1987, p. 32): "For gainsharing plans to work, a particular organizational structure and corporate culture are required—and these include an open discussion of the plan to gain employee acceptance, the establishment of cross-unit teams or task forces to develop the plan, and the adoption of suggestion systems."

As noted, the production environments in the experiments, as well as the incentive structures of production teams in industry, mirror social dilemmas. Indeed, the economy as a whole, viewed as an income-redistribution system, can be seen to incorporate elements of social dilemmas. There are often incentives for the least productive to free ride and accept their guaranteed payoffs or their share of the productivity gains of others. The extensive literature on cooperation in social dilemmas reveals that discussion (especially relevant discussion) increases cooperation (Messick and Brewer 1983, Dawes, McTavish, and Shaklee 1977, Dawes 1980). From that perspective it should not be surprising that increased participation in determining the content of the reward structure should increase the efforts of those who otherwise would have an incentive to free ride. And so potential solutions that are effective in overcoming free-rider tendencies in the laboratory are of interest in insulating redistributive systems from deleterious effects.

Our subjects' discussions parallel, and throw into clear relief, the widespread political debates in Western democracies regarding the appropriate limits for the welfare state. Concern for the poor and weak, a desire to recognize entitlements, and sensitivity to the need for incentives to maintain productivity, all enter into subjects' deliberations regarding a fair rule for implementing distributive justice. The choice of, and continued support for, the floor-constraint principle incorporates these competing normative and empirical demands.

The results provide an argument for meaningful participation in the democratic process that goes beyond the simple requirements of informed decision making and fairness. Meaningful participation on a broad scale might well have beneficial implications for productivity. It is not at all clear how such participation might be accomplished. Yet the potential impact of such participation should serve to entice us to examine means to achieve it.

A PARTING NOTE

We end with a challenge. If our results contain some potentially valid insights, the debate should now be joined by those who question their relevance. And it should be joined on empirical grounds. If cumulative progress is to be made, one needs to develop better experimental designs, broader sampling, and better controls. Our theorizing must be informed by empirical examination of the relevant facts. And then, perhaps, in Popper's spirit, new tests will overturn our results. Or, perhaps, the new work will lead to different results. A new path has been identified; where it may lead cannot be known unless it is explored.

Subject Handbook

This appendix consists of sample subject handbooks for the choice experiments in which subjects did not engage in production. Two of the five separate treatments are reflected here. One is the basic experiment, in which subjects stood to gain income and in which the exemplary income distributions did not have very large variances. The actual document consists of all text not in boldface. The second handbook presented is for the variation of the basic experiment in which all reference to justice was removed. It can be read by deleting all regular type in square brackets ([]) and replacing it with all **boldface** type in braces ({}). The two handbooks are identical except for the references to fairness and justice contained in the basic experiment but not in the variation.

Both handbooks include descriptions of the principles for redistributing payoffs, sample income distributions, sample problems, tests, four choice situations that provide subjects with experience in choosing principles and getting a random assignment to a payoff class, several measures of preferences for principles, and rules for discussion and decision making. This handbook does not contain the debriefing questionnaire.

This experiment deals with the [question: "What is a just distribution of income?" An individual's lifetime income is in part a result of many genetic and social accidents. The luckiest get the greatest talents and the highest rewards such as status and wealth. The least fortunate get the lowest abilities and opportunities, and receive the associated costs of poverty. Societies can deal with these inequities and risks by adopting income redistribution policies. This experiment deals with the justice of such policies.] {question of the distribution of monetary gains or losses among members of committees.} The experiment is divided into three parts.

In the first part of the experiment each of you will be introduced to a few [theories of justice.] {possible rules for distributing the monetary gains and losses among committee members.} To do this you will consider some examples and make some choices. These choices will have real monetary consequences for you. Your pay for the first part of the experiment will be based on your choices. You will have 1 hour for the first part. In this part you will be given a series of questions. These questions are merely to ensure that you have learned the concepts which are being used in the experiment. If you do not answer the questions correctly, then you *are to* go back to review the material and correct wrong answers. Once you have mastered the material, you can go on to make choices for which you will be paid. If you do not learn the material in a reasonable amount of time, you will not be able to earn as much money as possible since you must finish the first part of the experiment in 1 hour. But you *should* have plenty of time to finish this part of the experiment. Everyone will go on to the second part either after 1 hour or after everyone has finished Part I, whichever occurs first.

In the second part, you will all be asked, as a group, to discuss [notions of justice. After the discussion, you will be asked to reach a group decision on which principle of justice you like best. Your pay for Part II of the experiment will be based on the principle which the group chooses.] {possible rules for distributing monetary gains or losses. After the discussion, you will be asked to reach a group decision on which rule for distributing the money you like best. Your pay for Part II of the experiment will be based on the rule which the group chooses.}

In the third part, you will be asked some background questions about yourself. Upon completion of the third part you will receive the sum of your earnings from the two parts of the experiment by check. The money you receive is to be yours alone. No discussion or agreement to share earnings is permitted.

Throughout the experiment, we shall scale all examples and choices so that the monies can be thought of as average lifetime incomes. We then refer to these stakes as incomes. In Part I your actual stakes are equal to $1 for every $10,000 of income listed in the text.

PART I

[This experiment is concerned with the justice of different income distributions. Let us begin by discussing some ways of judging the justice of an income distribution.] {**This experiment is concerned with committee decisions about rules to distribute income among members of a society which *includes you*. Let us begin by discussing the effect of different rules on what you will get in the experiment.**} One way of judging [the justice of an income distribution] {**the effect of different rules on what you will get**} is to consider the overall pattern of income distribution. A number of [principles] {**rules**} have been suggested for [these sorts of judgments] {**adoption for the distribution of income**}, and we shall illustrate them by pointing out four such [principles.] {**rules.**} But there are obviously other possible alternatives. *You may well think of some alternatives yourself!*

To illustrate such principles consider the following four notions [of justice]:

1. Maximizing the Floor Income

[*The most just distribution of income is that which maximizes the floor (or lowest) income in the society.*] {***The best rule for distributing income is that which maximizes the floor (or lowest) income in the society.***}

This [principle] {rule} *considers only the* [welfare] {income} *of the worst-off individual in society.* In judging among income distributions, *the distribution which ensures the poorest person* {(who might be you)} the highest [income is the most just. No] {income, ensures that no} person's income can go up unless it increases the income of the people at the very bottom.

2. Maximizing the Average Income

[*The most just distribution of income*] {*The best rule for distributing incomes*} *is that which maximizes the average income in the society.*

For any society maximizing the average income maximizes the total income in the society. Since you don't know what you may get, this maximizes your average or mathematically expected income.

3. Maximizing the Average with a Floor Constraint of $———

[*The most just distribution of*] {*The best rule for distributing*} *income is that which maximizes the average income only after a certain specified minimum income is guaranteed to everyone.*

Such a [principle] {rule} insures that the attempt to maximize the average is constrained so as to ensure that individuals "at the bottom" receive a specified minimum. To choose this [principle] {rule} one must specify the value of the floor (lowest income).

4. Maximizing the Average with a Range Constraint of $———

[*The most just distribution of*] {*The best rule for distributing*} *income is that which attempts to maximize the average income only after guaranteeing that the difference between* [*the poorest and the richest individuals'*] {*smallest and the largest*} *incomes (i.e., the range of income) in the society is not greater than a specified amount.*

Such a [principle] {rule} ensures that the attempt to maximize the average does not allow income differences [between rich and poor] to exceed a specified amount. To choose this [principle] {rule} one must specify the dollar difference between the high and low incomes.

Of course, there *are* other possible [principles,] {rules,} and you may think of some of them.

Now that you have been familiarized with these four [principles,] {rules,} please answer the following questions:

Rank order, according to your preferences, the following 4 [principles of distributive justice] {rules for distributing income} by placing the letters (a), (b), (c), (d), signifying the [principles] {rules}, in the blanks below. Indicate ties by placing the tied [principles] {rules} in the same space.

most preferred ＿＿＿ ＿＿＿ ＿＿＿ ＿＿＿ least preferred

a. maximize the floor income
b. maximize the average income
c. maximize the average income, subject to a floor constraint
d. maximize the average income, subject to a range constraint

How do you feel about your ranking of these [principles?] {rules?} (Circle the appropriate answer.)

1. very unsure
2. unsure
3. no opinion
4. sure
5. very sure

To familiarize you with the sorts of choices you will be making, consider the following sample situation.

Sample Situation

Consider the following four income distributions (each of the money entries represents a yearly dollar income for a household):

	Income Distributions			
Income Class	*1*	*2*	*3*	*4*
High	$32,000	$28,000	$31,000	$21,000
Medium high	27,000	22,000	24,000	20,000
Medium	24,000	20,000	21,000	19,000
Medium low	13,000	17,000	16,000	16,000
Low	12,000	13,000	14,000	15,000
Average income				
Floor or low income	12,000	13,000	14,000	15,000
Range	20,000	15,000	17,000	6,000

[a] The average income was not given to the subjects at this point. It can be calculated only with knowledge of how many people will receive each level of income. We did not give the subjects any information about this.

You are to make a choice from among the four [principles of justice] {**rules**} which are mentioned above: (a) maximizing the floor, (b) maximizing the average, (c) maximizing the average with a floor constraint, and (d) maximizing the average with a range constraint. *If you choose (c) or (d), you will have to tell us what that floor or range constraint is before you can be said to have made a well defined choice.* Your choice of a [principle] {**rule**} will [select one of the four income distributions as the most just.] {**be applied to the income distributions above.**}

Only one of the income distributions is consistent with each rule. That means that your selection of a rule also selects one of the four income distributions as the one you prefer. Indicate your choice *of a [principle]* {**rule**} here:_____.

In making this choice, recall that your choice will yield you a payoff. How will your choice determine your pay? If, for example, you choose (a) to maximize the floor or low income, you will have picked that distribution (from the four in the sample question) which has the highest floor. (In this case distribution 4.) This ensures that you would get at least $15,000 if you were to be the worst off individual. This is the most that a member of the low income class could get from any of these distributions.

Let us say you choose a [principle] {rule} which leads to the selection of distribution 4: maximizing the floor or low income. After your choice has been made, five predetermined numbers will be used to determine your payoff. They represent the probability or chance that you will "be in" each of the five income classes and hence receive the payoffs associated with that income class. The numbers add up to one, and are each some fraction bigger than zero and smaller than one. Thus, the numbers can be thought of as the proportion of the population (of some hypothetical society) which receives that particular income level in the distribution. You will be assigned to an income class using these proportions. *You will then receive one dollar for each $10,000 received by a member of the income class you have been assigned to.*

To see how your payoff is calculated, again consider the illustration above and assume you have chosen to maximize the floor income. Suppose the distribution of (a fictitious) population over these income classes has been set at:

Income Class	Proportion of Population
high	5
medium high	10
medium	50
medium low	25
low	10

This means that you have a 5% chance of being assigned to the highest income class. Were you to be so assigned, you would get a payoff of $2.10—the highest in the distribution #4 (in this case, the distribution which maximizes the floor or low income). Similarly you have a 10% chance of being assigned to the medium high class, etc. If you were assigned to the medium class (in this example, the most likely, with a likelihood of 50%) you would get $1.90. *These assignments to income classes will be made randomly* by your drawing a piece of paper from a bag. You may think of them as "accidents of birth."

Now, what if you chose to maximize the average income? The average income in the society must be calculated by taking into account the proportion of the population which receives each particular income in the income distribution. Taking this into account, the average income for each of the income distributions is as stated in the following table:

	Income Distributions			
Income Class	*1*	*2*	*3*	*4*
High	$32,000	$28,000	$31,000	$21,000
Medium high	27,000	22,000	24,000	20,000
Medium	24,000	20,000	21,000	19,000
Medium low	13,000	17,000	16,000	16,000
Low	12,000	13,000	14,000	15,000
Average income	20,750	19,150	19,850	18,050
Floor or low income	12,000	13,000	14,000	15,000
Range	20,000	15,000	17,000	6,000

If you chose the [principle] {rule} of maximizing the average income, this would select distribution #1, which has an average income of $20,750. Therefore, on average, people selecting this [principle] {rule} in this example would receive $2.07.

In all of the subsequent situations you will be given the average income for each income distribution but will *not* be told the proportion of population in each income class. The proportions of the society in each income class *will vary* from one situation to another.

What if one chose to maximize the average with some constraint: say a floor constraint? How would this work? If you want to maximize the average while guaranteeing that no one receives an income below, let's say, $14,000, only those income distributions with a floor of $14,000 or more are acceptable: in this case distributions #3 and #4. Of these, distribution #3 has a higher average income and therefore maximizes the average with a floor constraint of $14,000. Notice that lowering the constraint to $13,000 allows us to consider distribution #2 as well. This does not affect which distribution would be picked, however, because #3 has a higher average than #2. Lowering it still further, to $12,000, would, on the other hand, allow distribution #1 to be considered *and selected* (since #1 has the highest average).

Finally, let us consider what happens if we choose to maximize the average income with a range constraint. The most restrictive range constraint applicable here is $6,000, which would lead to a selection of distribution #4. If one increased the permitted difference between the high and low incomes to $15,000, income distribution #2 would be allowable and chosen since it has the higher average income, etc.

Remember, the more demanding the constraint (i.e., the smaller the range or the higher the floor), the larger the number of income distributions which are ruled out.

When you are shown your payoff, you will also be shown what you would have gotten had you chosen any of the other three [principles.] {rules.} This will permit you to see the consequences of your choices.

Before you make any choices of [principles of justice,] {**rules of income distribution,**} you are required to answer some questions to test your understanding of the [principles of justice.] {**rules.**} You may refer to any part of the booklet in deciding on your answers. When you finish answering the questions, bring your answers to the moderator. If you make mistakes, you will be given chances to correct them—but do not erase any mistakes after the moderator has looked at them. The following information may help you to answer the questions:

A. The range is the difference between the highest and lowest values.
B. The floor is the lowest value.
C. If one chose to maximize the average "with a floor constraint" of $10,500, this means: one selects that income distribution with the highest average such that everyone gets at least $10,500.
D. If one chose to maximize the average "with a range constraint" of $10,000, this means: one selects that income distribution with the highest average such that the difference between the highest and lowest income is no more than $10,000.

Test

	Income Distributions			
Income Class	**1**	**2**	**3**	**4**
High	$30,000	$19,000	$26,000	$29,000
Medium high	25,000	18,000	20,000	22,000
Medium	20,000	16,000	18,000	18,000
Medium low	15,000	14,000	15,000	14,000
Low	10,000	13,000	11,000	12,000
Average income	20,000	16,000	18,000	19,000
Floor or low income	_____	_____	_____	_____
Range	_____	_____	_____	_____

1. In the blank space in the distributions write in the floor or low income for each distribution.

2. In the blank spaces in the distributions above write in the range for each distribution.

3. Indicate which distribution would be singled out [as the most just] by application of each of the following [principles.] {**rules.**}

   A. Maximization of the floor income would select distribution _____.

   B. Maximization of the average income would select distribution _____.

   C. Maximization of the average income with a floor constraint of $11,500 would select distribution _____.

   D. Maximization of the average income with a range constraint of $16,000 would select distribution _____.

4. If I were to choose to maximize the floor income, the lowest income I could get would be _____; the highest would be _____.

5. If I were to choose to maximize the average income, the lowest income I could get would be _____; the highest would be _____.

Please answer the following question, true or false:

6. After choosing a [principle of justice] {**rule about the distribution of income**}, my payoff will be determined by the probability of being in each income class and the luck of the draw. (Circle one: true or false.)

Please bring this paper to the moderator to be corrected.

Now that you have some acquaintance with the [principles of justice,] {**possible rules for distributing income,**} and before you begin making choices in the situations below, please indicate your preferences for the [principles.] {**rules.**} Rank them from most preferred to least preferred by placing the letters (a), (b), (c), and (d), corresponding to the [principles] {**rules**}, in the blank spaces below. Indicate ties by placing tied [principles] {**rules**} in the same blanks.

most preferred _____ _____ _____ _____ least preferred

   a. maximize the floor income
   b. maximize the average income
   c. maximize the average income, subject to a floor constraint
   d. maximize the average income, subject to a range constraint

How do you feel about your ranking of these [principles?] {**rules?**} (Circle the appropriate answer.)

1. very unsure
2. unsure
3. no opinion
4. sure
5. very sure

Choices with Payoffs

Situation A   Would you now please consider the income distributions below and choose a [*principle of justice*] {**rule**} which you feel would yield the best choice of an income distribution for the society. On your tally sheet place a check mark in the column labeled Situation A opposite your choice of [principle.] {**rule.**} Be sure to fill in the other information required if you choose to maximize with a constraint.

Remember, in making this choice, you will be determining a real money payoff for yourself.

To get your payoff recorded bring your tally sheet to the moderator.

DO NOT GO TO THE NEXT SITUATION UNTIL YOU HAVE TAKEN YOUR TALLY SHEET TO THE MODERATOR.

	Income Distributions			
Income Class	*1*	*2*	*3*	*4*
High	$28,000	$35,000	$30,000	$25,000
Medium high	25,000	30,000	29,000	22,000
Medium	20,000	25,000	28,000	19,000
Medium low	15,000	15,000	27,000	16,000
Low	12,000	10,000	6,000	13,000
Average income	20,000	23,500	26,000	19,000
Floor or low income	12,000	10,000	6,000	13,000
Range	16,000	25,000	24,000	12,000

Situation B Would you now please consider the income distributions below and choose a [*principle of justice*] {**rule**} which you feel would yield the best choice of an income distribution for the society. On your tally sheet place a check mark in the column labeled Situation B opposite your choice of [principle.] {**rule.**} Be sure to fill in the other information required if you choose to maximize with a constraint.

Remember, in making this choice, you will be determining a real money payoff for yourself.

To get your payoff recorded bring your tally sheet to the moderator.

DO NOT GO TO THE NEXT SITUATION UNTIL YOU HAVE TAKEN YOUR TALLY SHEET TO THE MODERATOR.

	Income Distributions			
Income Class	*1*	*2*	*3*	*4*
High	$17,000	$30,000	$40,000	$26,000
Medium high	16,000	25,000	30,000	24,000
Medium	15,000	20,000	25,000	22,000
Medium low	14,000	15,000	20,000	20,000
Low	13,000	12,500	8,000	11,000
Average income	14,800	19,200	23,550	20,900
Floor or low income	13,000	12,500	8,000	11,000
Range	4,000	17,500	32,000	15,000

Situation C Would you now please consider the income distributions below and choose a [*principle of justice*] {**rule**} which you feel would yield the best choice of an income distribution for the society. On your tally sheet place a check mark in the column labeled Situation C opposite your choice of [principle.] {rule.} Be sure to fill in the other information required if you choose to maximize with a constraint.

Remember, in making this choice, you will be determining a real money payoff for yourself.

To get your payoff recorded bring your tally sheet to the moderator.

DO NOT GO TO THE NEXT SITUATION UNTIL YOU HAVE TAKEN YOUR TALLY SHEET TO THE MODERATOR.

	Income Distributions			
Income Class	*1*	*2*	*3*	*4*
High	$100,000	$35,000	$30,000	$24,000
Medium high	30,000	30,000	25,000	23,000
Medium	20,000	25,000	23,000	22,000
Medium low	15,000	20,000	15,000	21,000
Low	13,000	8,000	12,000	11,000
Average income	19,500	22,350	20,000	20,710
Floor or low income	13,000	8,000	12,000	11,000
Range	87,000	27,000	18,000	13,000

Situation D   Would you now please consider the income distributions below and choose *a [principle of justice]* {rule} which you feel would yield the best choice of an income distribution for the society. On your tally sheet place a check mark in the column labeled Situation D opposite your choice of [principle.] {rule.} Be sure to fill in the other information required if you choose to maximize with a constraint.

Remember, in making this choice, you will be determining a real money payoff for yourself.

To get your payoff recorded bring your tally sheet to the moderator.

DO NOT GO TO THE NEXT SITUATION UNTIL YOU HAVE TAKEN YOUR TALLY SHEET TO THE MODERATOR.

Income Class	Income Distributions			
	1	**2**	**3**	**4**
High	$35,000	$30,000	$20,000	$30,000
Medium high	30,000	28,000	18,000	28,000
Medium	25,000	26,000	16,000	24,000
Medium low	20,000	24,000	14,000	20,000
Low	13,000	12,000	12,000	14,000
Average income	23,550	24,500	15,500	22,700
Floor or low income	13,000	12,000	12,000	14,000
Range	22,000	18,000	8,000	16,000

Now that you have been further familiarized with the four [principles,] {**rules,**} please answer the following question:

Rank order according to your preferences in following 4 [principles of justice] {**rules**} by placing the letters (a), (b), (c), (d), corresponding to the [principles] {**rules**}, in the blanks below. Indicate ties by placing the tied [principles] {**rules**} in the same space.

most preferred ＿＿＿ ＿＿＿ ＿＿＿ ＿＿＿ least preferred

a. maximize the floor income
b. maximize the average income
c. maximize the average income, subject to a floor constraint
d. maximize the average income, subject to a range constraint

How do you feel about your ranking of these [principles?] {**rules?**} (Circle the appropriate answer.)

1. very unsure
2. unsure
3. no opinion
4. sure
5. very sure

PART II

In this part of the experiment you, as a group, are to choose one [principle of justice] {**rule for the distribution of income**} for yourselves. This choice will determine the payoff you get in this part of the experiment. Your payoffs will be determined as follows. We have constructed a large set of payoff distribution schedules. Each schedule specifies five payoff amounts. The distributions need not resemble the distributions in Part I. THE STAKES IN THIS PART OF THE EXPERIMENT ARE MUCH HIGHER THAN IN THE FIRST PART. Your choice of [principle] {**rule**} will be used to pick out those distribution schedules which conform to your [principle.] {**rule.**} Thus, for example, if you picked the [principle] {**rule**} to maximize the average income, you would be saying that the group wants to pick out a distribution with the highest average income. If there is more than one distribution which has this maximum average income, one will be picked out for you as a group. *Each of you will then be randomly assigned an income from that distribution.* That is your payoff for Part II. Before the group votes on adopting a [principle] {**rule**} [of justice], there is to be a full and open discussion of the matter before the group. You must follow the procedures below for the discussion and voting phase.

Discussion Phase

You begin by having a group discussion about which [principle] {**rule**} you should adopt. The group can terminate this discussion anytime after 5 minutes. If after 5 minutes you feel nothing more can be gained by further discussion, you are to tell this to the moderator. Participants must agree *unanimously by secret ballot* that further discussion is unnecessary for discussion to be ended. You have whatever time you need, within reason, to discuss the issue. You *are not restricted*, in any way, *to the four* [*principles of justice*] {**rules**} mentioned above. Thus, you can discuss (and later adopt) other [principles.] {**rules.**} Any one of you can introduce and begin discussion of any [principle.] {**rule.**} But not just any rule is a [principle.] {**rule.**} There are two requirements which a rule must meet to be considered a [principle of justice] {**rule**}.

First, the rule *cannot use names.* For example, a rule which gives all to one *specified* person is not permitted because it specifies a *named* person. However, a rule which gives all the income to some *unspecified* person *is* permitted.

Second, only those rules which *always* lead to the choice of ["just distributions"] {**some income distributions**} from any set of alternatives is [a principle.] {**allowed.**} For example, strict equality is not a [principle] {**rule**} since it may not be achievable. But equality could be approximated by a [principle] {**rule**} to "minimize the range" in the distribution of income.

Finally, there are a few requirements you should bear in mind if you wish to adopt a [principle] {**rule**} which involves a constraint. You should think of dollar figures as annual family incomes in a democratic society of moderate scarcity.

If you wish to consider a range constraint, you must specify the dollar amount.

If you wish to consider a floor constraint, you are not in a position to know what floors are achievable for everyone. Of course there is a maximum achievable floor income in the set of income distributions. This means you have two ways of specifying a floor constraint: (1) You can specify an absolute dollar amount which you wish to have as a floor constraint. If that dollar amount is above the maximum floor achievable in our set of distributions, you will be assigned the income distribution with the highest achievable floor. (2) You can specify your floor constraint as a dollar amount below the maximum floor achievable in our distributions. This will guarantee the existence of such a distribution but you will not know what the absolute dollar amount of this floor is until after the voting has been completed.

Choice Phase

After your discussion you, as a group, are to vote to adopt a [principle of distributive justice] {rule}. Your voting will be according to the following procedure. The group will adopt a [principle] {rule} if, and only if, that [principle] {rule} is able to secure the *unanimous* support of the group against *all* other [principles] {rules} sketched above, plus any others which you have discussed. The [principles] {rules} are to be voted upon, two at a time. Only that [principle] {rule} which gets *unanimous* support in two-way contests against all other [principles] {rules} is actually adopted by the group. If no such proposal exists, then the group will have adopted no [principle.] {rule.} In that case, any member of the group can ask for extra discussion, which can be terminated at any time using the procedure described above. A new vote would follow.

Your payoffs in this section of the experiment will conform to the [principle] {rule} which you, as a group, adopt. If you, as a group, do not adopt any [principle] {rule}, then we will select one of the income distributions at random for you as a group. That choice of income distribution will conform to no particular characteristics.

Remember: Whatever income distribution is chosen, YOU WILL BE RANDOMLY PLACED IN AN INCOME CLASS IN THAT DISTRIBUTION, AND THAT DETERMINES THE MONEY YOU WILL GET.

Are there any questions? If so, please ask them now, or at any time during this part of the experiment.

Choices of Principles
by Experimental Type

The details of the choices of principles by experimental type are given in Table B1, where the types of experiments (rows) are related to the choices of principle (columns). (Excluded from the table are data from ten experiments in which groups were not asked to reach any decisions about a distributive principle.) The data come from eighty-eight experiments (400 people) in which there was a request for a group decision. In five of these, unanimity was not required.

Table B2 indicates that the distributions in each of the North American locations were rather smooth and unimodal. In Poland, however, we see two differences. Polish constraints were much higher relative to the notion of social poverty or hardship than they were in North America. And the distribution of constraints in Poland does not exhibit the symmetry of the North American distributions.

Table B1. Experiment Type and Group Choice of Principle

	No Consensus	Floor Constraint	Maximum Floor	Range Constraint	Maximum Income	Total Groups
Regular stakes with gain	7	23	1	2	1	34
Regular stakes with loss	0	11	0	0	5	16
High stakes with gain	0	6	0	1	1	8
High stakes with loss	0	4	0	1	1	6
Nonjustice	0	4	0	0	2	6
Production	0	15	0	3	0	18
Total	7	63	1	7	10	88

Table B2. Distribution of Floor Constraints Chosen in the Four Test Locations

Size of Constraint (thousands of dollars)	Florida	Manitoba	Maryland	Poland
		Each Digit Represents an Observation [a]		
2		0		
3			6	
4				
5			0	
6			001	
7		5		
8	0		005	
9	0			
10	000	00055	00000	
11	0	05	08	
12	05	000	000058	0
13	0		000	
14		5	00	4
15			07	
16				
17	2			
18				00
19				
20				
21				66
22				
23			4	
24				000

[a] The value is the number of hundreds of dollars above the thousand indicated in the left column. Thus, the 6 in the second row represents a floor set at $3,600.

Analyzing the Role of Background and Attitudinal Variables

The variables are listed below in more or less the order in which they appear in Chapter 5.

1. INCRED is a constructed variable measuring the general attitude toward income distribution. It is calculated as the sum of the responses to four questions (2–5) about income-distribution policy.

Questions 2–12 are all answered on a five-point scale: (1) disagree strongly, (2) disagree somewhat, (3) neither agree nor disagree, (4) agree somewhat, (5) agree strongly. The higher the score, the greater the agreement.

2. Relative equality of wealth is a good thing.
3. Government ought to have programs which give money to people like me when unavoidable events interrupt our ability to support ourselves.
4. A proper role of government is to modify the distribution of earned income.
5. Governments should ensure that all poor people can afford a relatively decent standard of living.
6. My expected monetary reward from this experiment was sufficient to affect my choices.
7. My reason for agreeing to participate in this experiment was to earn money.

8. My reason for agreeing to participate in this experiment was my interest in the project.

9. The greatest accomplishments in history were individual efforts.

10. In every country there are groups of people who are naturally inferior.

11. An individual's lifetime income is in part a result of many genetic and social accidents. The luckiest get the greatest talents and the highest rewards such as status and wealth. The least fortunate get the lowest abilities and opportunities, and receive the associated costs of poverty.

12. Life would hardly be worth living in a society in which I couldn't give someone else pleasure by my actions.

The scales for the following questions are indicated within the text describing each. For question 13 the answers were expressed as percentages on a 0–100 scale for each of the responses.

13. What percentage of your college expenses are met by each of the following: (a) parents' help, (b) income you earn, (c) trust monies, (d) scholarships, (e) loans, (f) spouse's help.

14. AVGSAL: average of the next three variables.

15. STARTSAL: What minimum annual income (in thousands of today's dollars [zlotys]) do you think you will find satisfactory as your starting salary for your first job after graduation?[1]

16. AGE35SAL: What minimum annual income do you think you will find satisfactory at age thirty-five?

17. AGE50SAL: Similar to AGE35SAL but at age fifty.

18. IDEOL: Rate your ideological preference on a scale from 1 (most conservative) to 5 (most liberal).

19. AVGSURE is the subject's average sureness of his or her rankings of the principles over the course of the experiment. Sureness ranges from 1 (for very unsure) to 5 (for very sure).

20. MAFCS1 is the score assigned to the subject's first ranking of the floor-constraint principle. It ranges from 30 for a first place (untied) to 0 (for a last place).

21. MAS1 and MARCS1 similarly represent the respective

---

1. The responses to the questions in Poland were in zloty and in North America were in dollars. The rules for currency conversion are discussed in Chapter 4.

scores of the principles of maximum income and range constraint. Their scores range on the same scale.

Attitudes toward risk were measured as a combination of the next two, equally weighted, questions:

22. Suppose someone offered to sell you a lottery ticket. In this lottery, one out of every four tickets will win $50. What is the most you would be willing to pay for it?
23. Suppose you have a lottery ticket. In this lottery one out of three tickets will win $50. If someone asked you to sell them the ticket, what is the minimum price you would sell it for?
24. For how many years of your life was your father employed before you were seven? (If you are not sure, estimate.) [An analogous question was asked about the subject's mother.]
25. Pro-Republican (and other party) attitudes. These were constructed as a composite from the following sorts of questions: Generally, you usually think of yourself as:
    a. Republican
    b. Democratic
    c. Independent
    d. No preference
    and (with regard to each party) you feel: [range from complete opposition (1) to complete support (5).]
26. For some people to succeed others must fail.
27. Describe your future career plans and aspirations [each was answered yes or no]: Public Service? Politics? Private Business? Private professional?

DETAILS OF DATA ANALYSIS

Table C1 gives details of statistically significant differences between North American and Polish subjects in attitudes toward income redistribution; in motivation for participating in the experiments; and in some attitudes toward life. As noted in Chapter 5, despite significant differences among locations on a number of variables, the subjects' motivations and attitudes not directly related to income distribution were not significant predictors of group choices of principles.

Nevertheless, there is a relationship between preferences for

Table C1. Attitudes and Motivations: Poland versus North America

	Income-Redistribution Attitudes	Motivation for Participation			Life Attitudes	
	(INCRED) [a]	Money Sufficient [b]	Earn Money [c]	Interest [d]	Life Not Worthwhile [e]	Income is Luck [f]
North America						
Mean	13.26	3.00	3.57	3.27	4.13	3.05
Standard deviation	3.19	1.30	1.30	1.13	0.98	1.23
Number of subjects	386[g]	388	389	389	389	388
Poland						
Mean	15.31	2.24	2.00	3.57	3.80	3.36
Standard deviation	3.02	1.29	1.30	1.30	1.09	1.34
Number of subjects	97	99	98	98	99	97
t	5.71	5.24	10.68	2.34	2.97	2.26
p	.001	.001	.001	.02	.003	.024

[a] A constructed variable to measure each subject's general attitude toward income distribution. It is the sum of 4 attitude questions 2 - 5 about income-distribution policy.

[b] Subject's expected monetary reward from this experiment was sufficient to affect choices.

[c] Subject's reason for agreeing to participate in this experiment was to earn money.

[d] Subject's reason for agreeing to participate in this experiment was interest in the project.

[e] Subject felt life would hardly be worth living in a society in which the subject couldn't give someone else pleasure by his or her actions.

[f] Subject felt an individual's lifetime income is in part a result of many genetic and social accidents: the luckiest get the greatest talents and the highest rewards such as status and wealth; the least fortunate get the lowest abilities and opportunities, and receive the associated costs of poverty.

[g] Ns may vary because of missing data.

principles and actual choices. The LOGIT analysis displayed in Table C2 shows that the group choice of principle can be thought of as a function of the set of preferences of the individual group members just prior to making the choice.[2] The first part of the table confirms that the rankings of principles are different among the groups choosing the three principles. In the second part one can see that the estimates of the coefficients can be accepted with considerable confidence. And predictions on the basis of the model are quite significant as measured by the chi-square test. This LOGIT model yields a chi-square of 22.28 with 4 degrees of freedom, which indicates that the probability of the underlying model being significantly different from the null hypothesis is better than .999.

Table C3 demonstrates that indirect measures of preferences for principles (in this case, attitudes toward income distribution) can be used as modest predictors of group choices. The constructed index of support for income redistribution produces a nearly significant model to explain the choices. Of course, an index of support for income distribution in general should be expected to provide a weaker explanation than a direct measure of preferences for principles.

BACKGROUND VARIABLES AND PREFERENCES

In Chapter 5 we discuss some possible threats to the validity of our results. We have seen that choices could not be explained by background factors but were explicable by direct and indirect measurements of preferences for principles of redistribution. A subordinate threat to the validity of the experiments might emerge were we able to demonstrate an indirect effect of background characteristics. It might be possible to explain either preferences or attitudes toward income redistribution via background variables. Were that true, it might be arguable that

2. Note that in this case the observations are group choices, and hence the data used to explain the choices are the aggregate (mean) levels of support for the principles by the group members.

Table C2. Individual Preferences for Principles and Group Choice ($\underline{N} = 79$)

Variable	Maximum Income	Floor Constraint	Range Constraint
Constant	1.00	1.00	1.00
Average score for maximum income	22.28	16.22	16.50
Average score for floor constraint	20.95	24.50	18.92

Parameter	Estimate	Standard Error	t	p
Model for Maximum Income				
Constant	-15.82	5.95	-2.66	.005
Average score for maximum income	0.47	0.17	2.76	.005
Average score for floor constraint	0.37	0.17	2.24	.025
Model for Floor Constraint				
Constant	-10.12	4.93	-2.05	.025
Average score for maximum income	0.24	0.14	1.67	.050
Average score for floor constraint	0.40	0.15	2.71	.005

Note: In this analysis all groups that chose the floor constraint, maximum income, or the range constraint are included. LOGIT generates models only for the floor constraint and maximum income.

Table C3. Individual Attitudes toward Income Distribution & Group Choices (N = 79)

Variable	Maximum Income	Floor Constraint	Range Constraint
Constant	1.00	1.00	1.00
Mean Support for income redistribution	12.27	13.74	13.64

Parameter	Estimate	Standard Error	t	p
Model for Maximum Income				
Constant	7.01	4.28	1.63	>.05
Support for income redistribution	-0.50	0.32	-1.55	>.05
Model for Floor Constraint				
Constant	1.87	3.46	0.54	>.10
Support for income redistribution	0.03	0.25	0.14	>.10

Note: In this analysis all groups that chose the floor constraint, maximum income, or the range constraint are included. LOGIT generates models only for the floor constraint and maximum income.

our experimental conditions do not generate conditions of impartial reasoning. In other words, if the predictors of choice were themselves explicable via characteristics of the subjects, the operationalization of impartiality might be flawed.

To test for this possibility we ran regressions on the preference scores of the principles as a function of the background characteristics of the subjects. We also attempted to predict the subjects' attitudes toward income redistribution on this basis. To simplify matters we concentrated the analysis on the two principles that were chosen with any significant frequency: the floor constraint and maximum income.

Having no explicit theory regarding the relationship between background characteristics and preferences, and desiring to uncover any strong relationships, we surveyed all possible relationships. Consequently, correlations between possible explanatory factors and individuals' scores on the two principles at the start of the experiment were calculated.[3]

Surprisingly, most of the variables that correlate significantly at a .1 level or better (see Table C4) are associated with only one principle (maximum income). Only four are related to support of both principles: (1) the number of years of father's employment prior to age seven; (2) the annual income (in thousands of today's dollars) thought to be minimally satisfactory at age fifty; (3) one's attitude toward whether government should ensure that all poor people can afford a relatively decent standard of living; and (4) the index of the cluster of attitudes toward income redistribution.

The correlations in the table give an indication of possible effects of background variables on preferences, but determining the strength of the combined effects requires calculation of a regression model. A stepwise regression was used to identify the variables that most strongly affect the support of the

3. Because the principles were "competitors" in the rankings of the individuals, the scores for the two principles cannot be independent. Hence any variables that strongly affect one set of scores would be expected to also affect the other (although negatively).

Table C4. Significant Correlations between Background Factors and Initial Support for Leading Principles

Variables	Floor Constraint		Maximum Income	
	Pearson's R	p	Pearson's R	p
Years father was employed	.13	.012	-.11	.029
Income-redistribution attitudes	.09	.050	-.29	.000
Minimum salary at age 50	-.08	.089	.10	.026
Government should insure against poverty	.19	.000	-.24	.000
Years mother was employed			-.11	.046
Ideology (+ = liberal)			-.14	.006
Relative equality is good			-.23	.000
Money enough to affect choice			.09	.049
Government ought to help helpless			-.17	.000
Some groups are inferior			.11	.019
Pro-Republican party			.21	.000
Some must fail			.09	.040
Lifetime income = luck			-.20	.000
Plans private professional career	-.11	.019		
Percentage of expenses met by loans	.09	.046		
Joined for the money	-.09	.046		
Joined out of interest	.11	.019		

subjects for the two principles.[4] (See Table C5.) We found that, at best, we could explain only a small proportion of the variance in the subjects' support of these principles on the basis of their backgrounds. Only 2.9 percent of the variance in the floor-constraint principle and 3.5 percent of the variance in the maximum-income principle were explicable. The best fitting models identified only three variables of any significance, but the low levels of variance explained lead us to conclude that the background factors we tapped had negligible impact on preferences for the principles.

A similar analysis was done for the later measures of support for the various principles, and a few speculative conclusions can be drawn from the changes in support over the course of the experiments. As the experiment progressed, the task of choosing a principle and its implications must certainly have become clearer to the subjects. If, therefore, later stages showed high and significant correlations between background factors and subjects' preferences, it would be strong presumptive evidence for the encroachment of individual factors on impartial reasoning. Subjects would presumably be projecting more of their self-knowledge into the content of their choices. This was not the case. To the contrary, the strength of the relationships between preferences and the initial predictor variables diminished over the course of the experiments.

In addition, new variables entered in as predictors as the subjects progressed through the experiment. Subjects seemed to be orienting themselves forward in time (from fathers' employment to future career and income aspirations) as the experiment unfolded. But the explantory power of all significant variables declined by about 2 percent in each case, and so not much of the variance in preference for principles is ever explained.

The effect of location on support for a floor constraint is also

---

4. Because some variables were not measured in Poland, some choices had to be made. Specifically, we used the grand mean value for the employment of the father from the rest of the cases for the Polish data so as not to lose the Polish cases in the regression model. This still left 112 missing cases.

Table C5. Regression Models of Background Variables Explaining Support for the
Principles

Dependent variable: Initial support for floor constraint

Model: Initial support for floor constraint = 16.22 + .77*(Interest in project) +
.04*Loans + .72*(Father's employment)

Number of subjects: 371
r = .193
Adjusted r² = .029

Variable	Coefficient	Standard Error	Coefficient	t	p(2tail)
Constant	16.23	2.84	0.00	5.72	.000
Interest in project	0.77	0.35	0.11	2.19	.029
Loans	0.04	0.02	0.11	2.18	.030
Father's employment	0.72	0.39	0.09	1.83	.068

Analysis of Variance

Source	Sum of squares	df	Mean square	F Ratio	p
Regression	820.56	3	273.52	4.73	.003
Residual	21214.75	367	57.81		

Table C5. Regression Models of Background Variables Explaining Support for the Principles (Continued)

Dependent Variable: Initial Support for Maximizing the Average

Model: Initial Support for Maximizing the Average = 24.25 - 1.19*(Ideological preference) - 1.06*(Father's Employment) + .72*(Inferior groups)

Number of subjects: 378
r = .207
Adjusted r² = .035

Variable	Coefficient	Standard Error	Coefficient	t	p(2tail)
Constant	24.25	3.89	0.00	6.23	.000
Ideological preference	-1.19	0.51	-0.12	-2.34	.020
Father's employment	-1.05	0.48	-0.11	-2.21	.028
Inferior groups	0.72	0.35	0.11	2.07	.039

Analysis of Variance

Source	Sum of squares	df	Mean square	F Ratio	p
Regression	1604.45	3	534.82	5.58	.001
Residual	35850.84	374	95.86		

of interest. Canadians were the most supportive of the principle, Floridians least. Even so, however, location can account for only 1.5 percent of the variance. When location is included as a categorical variable, the overall explained variance of support for the floor constraint rises to only 6.0 percent for a floor constraint and 4.6 percent for maximum income. Regression models attempting to explain preferences for principles just prior to the decision yield similarly low explanatory power.

One is drawn to the conclusion that although there are some relationships between a few background variables and support for the principles, there appears to be an underlying uniformity. And the uniformity is driven by the experimental stimulation of impartiality. The floor-constraint principle obtains wide support in all locations and across all measured characteristics. Under approximations of the conditions prescribed by philosophers, it has broad-based appeal.

If direct preferences cannot be explained by background factors, perhaps attitudes toward income redistribution can. Parallel to our previous analysis, we can develop a multiple-regression model to explain how overall support for income redistribution varies as a function of the differences in the individual characteristics noted.[5]

The stepwise linear-regression model to explain the individual's composite attitude toward redistribution (INCRED) is shown in Table C6. Here we see that when we searched for the strongest fit using all the variables available, we were still able to explain only 13 percent of the variance. And many of the variables on which Polish and North American subjects differed did not play a significant role in the explanation and hence are omitted. The result is highly significant, but not powerful. Note that two of the "deep-value" questions come into play here: (1) "Life would hardly be worth living in a society in which I couldn't give someone else pleasure by my actions." (2) "An individual's lifetime income is in part a result of

5. One major limitation of this method is that because all the variables correlating with our measure of support for income redistribution also vary as a function of the location, some of the effect is spurious.

Table C6. Regression Model of Background Variables Explaining Support for Redistribution

Dependent variable: index of support for income redistribution

Model: index of support for income redistribution = 5.23 + 0.1(age) + 0.00(acceptable starting salary) + 0.01(university cost paid by parents) + 0.02(university cost paid by loans) + 0.66(life hardly worth living) + 0.62(income result of luck)

Number of subjects: 456
Multiple R = .376
Adjusted R² = .130

Variable	Coefficient	Standard Error	Standard Coefficient	t	p (2-tail)
Constant	5.23	1.24	.00	4.21	.001
Age	0.09	0.04	.01	2.13	.034
Acceptable starting salary	0.00	0.00	.16	3.59	.000
University cost paid by parents	0.01	0.00	.11	2.35	.019
University cost paid by loans	0.02	0.01	.09	1.92	.055
Life hardly worthwhile	0.66	0.15	.20	4.58	.001
Income result of luck	0.62	0.12	.23	5.32	.001

Analysis of Variance

Source	Sum of Squares	df	Mean Square	F	p
Regression	693.28	6	115.55	12.34	.001
Residual	4,203.37	449	9.36		

many genetic and social accidents. The luckiest get the greatest talents and the highest rewards such as status and wealth. The least fortunate get the lowest abilities and opportunities, and receive the associated costs of poverty."

The details of the statistical model are given in Table C6. It would appear that the regression is statistically robust and not likely to be a function of peculiar chance happenings (the level of significance is a solid .001). But underlying differences in individual characteristics do not explain much of the difference in attitude toward income redistribution.

The regressions, taken together, point to the difficulty of explaining individual preferences for principles of income redistribution and for income redistribution in general. This failure is further supportive evidence for the notion that the group choices reflect the results of impartial reasoning. It reinforces the notion that the experimental conditions (1) decouple antecedent individual background factors from interests, and (2) generate sufficiently serious incentives to induce impartial reasoning.

Analyzing the Effect of Location on the Level of Floor Constraint

Not all variations of experimental conditions were run in each North American locale. In comparing treatments we must compare one experimental treatment in Maryland with another in Florida, and so forth. If this procedure is to be valid, a prior question must be disposed of: Is there a direct and significant effect of location within North America on the level of the constraint chosen? Only if we can answer in the negative are we free to proceed with the pairwise comparison of experimental treatments. The most direct way of answering this question is to see whether the means (see Table B2) of the constraints at each location differ significantly from one another. Fortunately (for subsequent analysis) the answer is straightforward: they do not (see Table D1). Given the relative homogeneity of constraints chosen across locations, we are justified in asking whether experimental type makes any difference in the level of constraint chosen.

Table D1. Mean Floor Constraints by Location in North America

$F = 0.276$ $p = .760$			
	Florida	*Manitoba*	*Maryland*
Number of groups	10	13	29
Mean	$11,272	$10,269	$10,983

Analyzing Changes
in Support for Principles
by Rankings

The analysis in the body of Chapter 7 offers evidence of movement over the course of the experiments. But the changes are not analyzed statistically. We can use our numerical scoring techniques to examine changes in the support for principles, including all of the ranking data—that is, we can take into account second-, third-, and fourth-place rankings as well. We do this in Table E1 by assigning weights of 30 to first-place rankings, 20 to second, and so forth, and constructing an index of support for each principle. Over the course of the discussion and collective-choice period, only the floor-constraint principle showed any increase in support, and it is statistically significant. All the others showed decreases, although, it should be noted, the drop in support for maximum income is not significant—that is, although maximum income had a lower score as a result of the discussion and group decision, it is not significantly lower. How can that result square with the reported loss of 28 of its 105 first-place rankings over that period? The answer lies in gains in its second- and third-place rankings against the two least popular principles. It moved into a solid second place.

Thus, the most popular principle gains at the expense of all others, and the second most popular gains at the expense of the two least popular. This is further evidence for the impact of the experimental treatment on individual preferences.

Table E1. Changes in Subjects' Rankings of Principles: Before and After the Group's Decision

| | Mean Score | | | | |
	Pre Decision	Post decision	F	p	N
Maximum floor	8.21	7.47	5.07	.025	419
Maximum income	16.44	15.97	1.92	.167	417
Floor constraint	24.18	25.95	28.46	.000	420
Range constraint	11.34	10.59	4.99	.026	418

Production Documents

CHANGES IN THE HANDBOOK

The basic experimental handbook was changed for the production experiments. Here we reproduce the text for the production experiments requiring unanimous choice. The following text was added to the beginning of the booklet:

This experiment deals with the question: "What is a just distribution of income?" An individual's lifetime income is in part a result of many genetic and social accidents. The luckiest get the greatest talents and the highest rewards such as status and wealth. The least fortunate get the lowest abilities and opportunities, and receive the associated costs of poverty. Societies can deal with these inequities and risks by adopting income redistribution policies. This experiment deals with the justice of such policies. The experiment is divided into three parts.

In the first part of the experiment each of you will be introduced to a few theories of just income distribution. You will have an hour for the first part, during which time you will be asked to answer some questions on the material. You will be paid 50 cents for every question you answer correctly on the test on this material the first time you take the test. These questions are merely to ensure that you have learned the concepts which are being used in the experiment. If you do not answer the questions correctly, then you *are to go back to review the material and correct wrong answers.* Once you have mastered the material you can try the missed questions again in another test, this time getting 25 cents for each correct answer. Obviously, you will not be able to earn as much money as possible if you do not do well on the test. Everyone will go on to the second part after 1 hour, or after everyone has finished Part I, whichever occurs first.

In the second part, you will all be asked, as a group, to discuss notions of justice. After the discussion, you will be asked to reach a group decision on which principle of justice you like best. Your "take home" pay for Part III of the experiment will be partially based on the principle which the group chooses.

In the third part, you will be required to perform some tasks to earn some money. Your earned income will then be taxed or supplemented so that the final distribution of income in this part is in accordance with the principle adopted by the group.

In the last part, you will be asked some background questions about yourself. Upon completion of the third part you will receive the sum of your earnings from the earlier parts of the experiment by check. The money you receive is to be yours alone. *No discussion or agreement to share your final pay is permitted. Any such discussions may void the experiment and lead to your earning nothing!*

[This next material substitutes for the sample-situation section of the basic experimental handbook.]

Here you can see that the amount that you would be able to keep would depend upon the distribution chosen. Similarly, at the bottom of the income ladder, you would be affected by the choice as shown on the low-income class line:

Income Class	Income Distributions			
	1	*2*	*3*	*4*
Low	1,000	2,250	4,500	8,000

It is one thing to make one's choice of an income distribution principle when one is fully aware of one's individual talents and place in society. It is quite another one to do so without such knowledge. Later you will be earning money by working at a task we have designed. You do not know how well you will be able to perform that task, how much income you will generate, and hence in which income class you will be. Recall that in the next part of the experiment you will try to reach a decision, with the other group members, as to which principle will govern the actual payments which will be made to each of you as a member of the group. Thus, your choice of a principle of income distribution will, to a great degree, determine how much you will be paid.

Precisely how will the selection of a principle relate to your earnings? To know this you must understand how your earned income will be redistributed on the basis of the principle chosen. Let us go over the four principles listed above, and illustrate how income would be redistributed to be in conformity with the principles.

1. Maximizing the floor requires that some of the income of persons who earn above the floor is used to increase the minimum income received in the group.

   If the amount of income in the group were fixed, the minimum could be maximized by having an equal division of the total income. Any less equal division of the income would stem from those who receive more getting it at the cost of those who receive less. When income is not tied to work, this may be true, but in general income IS tied to work.

   When there is a link between income and work, some people feel that there should be a link between *more* or *better* work and more income. Most supporters of this position argue that if there were an absolutely egalitarian income distribution there would be less work, less production, and hence less income. This could lead to less income for those at the bottom. Thus, to maximize the floor some people have argued that one needs to keep *some* incentives for productive work.

In the case of this experiment, your income is going to be tied to work. Hence, in keeping with this line of thinking, we preserve some of the income differences, but reduce them. In this experiment, choosing to maximize the floor leads us to set the floor at 80% of the mean. We do this by taxing the incomes earned by everyone else enough to raise the floor to the level required. We tax each of the individuals who earned more than 80% of the floor the same percentage of their incomes above the 80% floor. Thus the percentage of income which would be taxed away depends upon the amount of income needed to be transferred to the low income recipient.

2. Maximizing the average, we assume, means giving everyone as much incentive to produce as possible. We interpret this to mean that there will be no redistribution and, hence, no taxation.

3. Maximizing the average with a floor constraint also requires a tax system.

   In this case, all the incomes above the chosen floor are taxed at the same percentage rate, set so that it will raise enough income to raise the floor to the level required. Thus, each person's ranking—by income—above the floor stays the same, but the differences are compressed because of the taxes.

   One complication must be considered here. Since the idea is to continue having incentives to maintain high productivity and income, we insist that if the average income is so close to the floor that the floor is higher than 8/10 of the average income, then the floor is set at .8 of the average. This ensures that some minimal level of incentive is maintained and that the floor can never be higher under this principle than it could be if one were merely to maximize the income of the poorest member of the group.

4. Maximizing the average with a range constraint means that the difference between the highest and lowest income is restricted in accordance with the principle chosen. All the incomes that are "too low" (that is: the range between them and the top income is bigger than the acceptable limit) would

receive additional income raised by taxing the others. All others would be taxed so that the money raised, when transferred to the individuals with the low incomes, would reduce the range to the required level. This will keep the average income unchanged and keep the income differences between the individuals in the same proportion as they were before taxes. But this does restrict the range. To illustrate, imagine that persons in a society have earned incomes of $1,000, $5,000, $7,000, $11,000, $101,000. Then the average income is $25,000 and the range of earned income (between $1,000 per year and $101,000) is $100,000. If that society had a principle to maximize the average while restricting the range to $50,000, all four low income individuals would require transfers to reduce the range to within $50,000. The average would stay the same ($25,000), but the income differences would all be cut in half, so that the new distribution would be: $13,000; $15,000; $16,000; $18,000; and $63,000.

(You can choose to have an egalitarian distribution by restricting the range to zero.)

Before you are permitted to join with the other members of the group to choose a principle of justice, you are required to answer some questions to test your understanding of the principles of justice. You will be paid 50 cents for each numbered question answered correctly. You may refer to any part of the booklet in deciding on your answers. When you finish answering the questions, bring your answers to the moderator. If you make mistakes, you will be given chances to take another test—and show us that you have learned the material. But in the second test you will be paid only 25 cents per right answer, and you will only be asked to answer questions about material you did not master at first.

[The booklet continued with the information useful for the test.]

[The following are the texts of the tests used for the production experiments.]

Name _____ Number right _____

Below is a chart in which there are four numbered columns. Each column represents one possible income distribution in a hypothetical society. In this society there are 5 levels of income. In each of the columns, the first five rows represent the income which would be received by families at each income level. Look at column one: the richest families would each receive $36,000 were the income distribution of column 1 chosen for the society. In each of these columns the sixth row of numbers represents the average income in the society.

Income Class	Income Distributions			
	1	2	3	4
High	$36,000	$69,000	$29,000	$146,000
Medium high	25,000	48,000	20,000	22,000
Medium	15,000	36,000	18,000	8,000
Medium low	8,000	14,000	5,000	4,000
Low	1,000	13,000	1,000	2,000
Average income	17,000	36,000	14,600	36,400
Floor or low income	_____	_____	_____	_____
Range	_____	_____	_____	_____

1. In the blank space in the distributions write in the floor income and the range for each distribution.
2. Indicate which distribution would be singled out as the most just by application of each of the following principles.
    Maximization of the floor would select distribution _____.
    Maximization of the average income would select
        distribution _____.

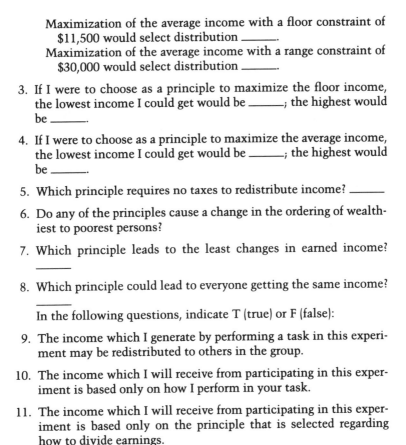

Maximization of the average income with a floor constraint of $11,500 would select distribution _____.

Maximization of the average income with a range constraint of $30,000 would select distribution _____.

3. If I were to choose as a principle to maximize the floor income, the lowest income I could get would be _____; the highest would be _____.

4. If I were to choose as a principle to maximize the average income, the lowest income I could get would be _____; the highest would be _____.

5. Which principle requires no taxes to redistribute income? _____

6. Do any of the principles cause a change in the ordering of wealthiest to poorest persons?

7. Which principle leads to the least changes in earned income? _____

8. Which principle could lead to everyone getting the same income? _____

In the following questions, indicate T (true) or F (false):

9. The income which I generate by performing a task in this experiment may be redistributed to others in the group.

10. The income which I will receive from participating in this experiment is based only on how I perform in your task.

11. The income which I will receive from participating in this experiment is based only on the principle that is selected regarding how to divide earnings.

12. The group is going to choose a principle of justice which will govern how the earnings of the group members are to be divided.

13. Any discussion, during the experiment, of a *postexperiment agreement to share earnings* is strictly against the rules of this experiment and can lead to my earning zero.

Bring this paper to the moderator to be corrected.

Now that you have some acquaintance with the principles of justice, and before you begin to work toward a choice in the group, please indicate your preferences for the principles. Rank them from most preferred to least preferred by placing the letters (a), (b), (c), and (d) corresponding to the principles in the blank spaces below. Indicate ties by placing tied principles in the same blanks.

most preferred _____ _____ _____ least preferred

a. maximize the floor income
b. maximize the average income
c. maximize the average income, subject to a floor constraint
d. maximize the average income, subject to a range constraint

How do you feel about your ranking of these principles? (Circle the appropriate answer.)

1. very unsure
2. unsure
3. no opinion
4. sure
5. very sure

[This next material substitutes for the Part II section of the handbook.]

In this part of the experiment you, as a group, are to choose one principle of justice for yourselves. This choice will govern the distribution of incomes to you as a group (that is, determine the payoff you get) in the experiment. Your payoffs will be determined as follows.

You will be assigned tasks and earn money in the jobs. Your earnings from the jobs will then be reallocated so as to conform to the principle you have chosen to govern income distribution. In order to reassign the earnings, we may have to impose taxes in accordance with the schemes outlined in the first part of the experiment. There will be a number of production and pay periods.

Before the group votes on adopting a principle of justice, there is to be a full and open discussion of the matter before the group. You must follow the procedures below for the discussion and voting phase.

[This next material substitutes for the discussion-phase section of the handbook.]

You begin by having a group discussion about which principle you should adopt. The group can terminate this discussion anytime after 5 minutes. If after 5 minutes you feel nothing more can be gained by further discussion, you are to tell this to the moderator. PARTICIPANTS MUST AGREE UNANIMOUSLY BY SECRET BALLOT THAT FURTHER DISCUSSION IS UNNECESSARY FOR DISCUSSION TO BE ENDED. You have whatever time you need, within reason, to discuss the issue. You *are not restricted*, in any way, *to the four principles of justice* mentioned above. Thus, you can discuss (and later adopt) other principles. Any one of you can introduce and begin discussion of any principle. But not just any rule is a principle. There are two requirements which a rule must meet to be considered a principle of justice.

First, the rule *cannot use names.* For example, a rule which gives all the income to one *specified* person is not permitted. However, a rule which gives all the income to some *unspecified* person *is* permitted.

Secondly, there are a few requirements you should bear in mind if you wish to adopt a principle which involves a constraint. You should think of dollar figures as annual incomes for a household in a democratic society of moderate scarcity.

If you wish to consider a range constraint, you must specify the dollar amount.

If you wish to consider a floor constraint, you are not in a position to know what floors will actually be *achievable* on the basis of the earnings of the group. We interpret a floor constraint as follows:

You can specify an absolute dollar amount which you wish to have as a floor constraint. If that dollar amount is above the maximum floor achievable given the group's earnings, we will set the floor at 80% of the average income.

The floor income can be viewed as the minimum income a head of an average household is guaranteed each year.

[The next material substitutes for the choice-phase section of the handbook.]

After your discussion you, as a group, are to vote to adopt a principle of distributive justice. Your voting will be according to the following procedure. THE GROUP WILL ADOPT A PRINCIPLE IF, AND ONLY IF, THAT PRINCIPLE IS ABLE TO SECURE THE UNANIMOUS SUPPORT OF THE GROUP AGAINST ALL OTHER PRINCIPLES SKETCHED ABOVE, PLUS ANY OTHERS WHICH YOU HAVE DISCUSSED. The principles are to be voted upon two at a time. Only that principle which gets unanimous support in two-way contests against all other principles is actually adopted by the group. If no such proposal exists, then the group will have adopted no principle. In that case, any member of the group can ask for extra discussion, which can be terminated at any time using the procedure described above. A new vote would follow.

Your payoffs in this section of the experiment will conform to the principle which you, as a group, adopt. We will translate your earnings at the job into annual income to apply your rule. We do this by calculating how much you would earn in a year, given your rate of earnings during the period you are working. If you, as a group, do not adopt any principle, then we will select a principle at random which will be applied to your earnings in the next part of the experiment.

Are there any questions? If so, please ask them now or at any time during this part of the experiment.

SPELLING DOCUMENTS

We reproduce here the three texts that the subjects corrected and the accompanying instructions. The instructions paragraph and heading stayed the same on each of the three separate sheets on which the corrections were made. We rotated the texts across subjects so that each text was used first one-third of the time.

NAME _____ Net Number Right _____

Instructions: You are to correct the spelling errors in the selection below. Do this by *circling the word* which you think is incorrectly spelled **and** *correcting it in the left margin.* No money can be earned unless you follow both of these instructions! You will be paid as follows: $.25 for each of the first 4 errors found; $1.50 for each of the next 4 errors found; and $3 for any more errors found. You have only 4 minutes[1] for this task. Any correct spellings which you identify as incorrect and change to an incorrect spelling will be subtracted from your total number of corrections. When you have completed this task, or time runs out, bring your paper to the monitor for scoring. Each of you has a different selection.

[Text #1] Let us now approach another exceadingly important aspec of this body of theory which relates to but goes beyond these main traditions. The emphasis on the importance of normative references as defining the situation for motivated and meaningful action has been noted. On the one hand, Weber, with reference to the cultural level, and Durkhem to the social, then came to the important conception of common normative elements, especially beliefs and values for Weber and the conscience colective for Durkheim. From these starting points it has gradually come to be understood that what I have called institusionalization and internalization (with reference to personality of the individual) of these normative elements constitute the primary focus of the control of action in social systems, threw processes whose general nature has come to be much better understood in recent years than preaviously.

The first aspect of this better understanding has come mainly from outside the behavoral sciences, namely from the

1. Subjects were given only three minutes for the second and third rounds of work.

biological analysis of self-regulating systems and from the engineering analysis and design of information-processing and automaticly regulated systems. The biological model goes back at least to the conception of the constansy of the internal environment of the organism as self-regulating by Claude Bernard, especially as further developed by W. B. Cannon in his concept of homeostatis. It has, however, received an enormous recent impitus by the extension of such conceptions to the field of cellulur biology and biochemistry in the new knowledge about the mechanisms of heredity, both of species and of individual cells, through the complex molecules of DNA and RNA. The developments from engineering have of course involved the analysis of communications systems, computers and automation.

[Text #2] All of these developments have introduced a new perspective. It is that of the importance of the mechanisms responsable for the implementation of patterns for "plans" which, operating with low energy, can control systems of much higher energy. It has become clear that the outputs of such systems are closely analogus to symbols having meanings, and indeed there has been established a direct bridge between information theory and linguistics. It is above all across this bridge that contact has been made by these natural science conceptions with the historic problem areas of the disiplines dealing with human social behavior. The key proposition, one might say, is that social interaction operates overwelmingly through linguistic communication and that language and other simbolic media constitute the primary mechanisms of its control articulating as they must with the motivational mechanisms, internal to the personality, which are involved in intensional linguistic expression and in turn those involved with stiumlus, through reception of meanings, to overt action.

The bearing of this development on the ancient controversy over the relative significanse of Idealfactoren and Realfactoren in the social prosess should be evident. This very old problem presents quite clearly a false dilemma in the sense that the nineteenth century argument over hereditary versus environment in the biological sense involved a false dilema. Quite clearly both sets of factors are essential to any adequate analysis of proceses in social systems, including those by which concrete structures come to be changed from one for into another. This bald statment is not, however, taken alone, very helpful. It is necessary to be in a position to be much more specific about just what the changes are and just how (i.e., by what proceses) they occur.

[Text #3] The relations among these theoreticaly essential elements in the analysis of prosess must be established by a specifically socio-logical articulasion between the cultural categories of meaning and the psychological categories of motivation, an articulasion which has been taking shape in the conception of institutionalized values and norms on the one hand, of roles and colectivities on the other, as the primary structural components of social systems within which meaningful motivated action can be analized. In one sense systimatic attention to this type of analysis of motivated action is no longer a matter of "structural-functional" theory in the simpler meaning of that concept. It establishes a new level on which I think it safe to say the parallel terms are not structure and function but structure and prosess. The concept of function then becomes the common point of reference for the formulation of problems, which is common to both the others and which binds them together in terms of their relevence to the master concept of system.

By these criteria Max Weber was not in a strict sense a structural-functional theorist—not as strict as Durkhem or Radcliffe-Brown. He did, however, think in very similar terms, but without such strict refrence to the concept of a social system. His greater emphasis on motivated action and the coginate conception of process, however, has made his work a very important bridge to a more process-oriented sociology. The firm foundation in a systematic conception of a functionaly ordered and diferentiated system outlined above has, however, made it possible to make the Weberian type of analysis more rigorous and hence fruitfull than it originally was.

PAY DOCUMENTS

Name _____   SSN _____

Test 1: _____ = no. rt. /2 = $_____

Test 2: _____ = no. rt. /4 = $_____

Rule selected for group: _____

Task 1:   Your production: _____; group production: _____; On this basis, your

earned income (at a yearly rate) was:before redistribution: $_____;

after redistribution: $_____

Task 2:   Your production: _____; group production: _____; On this basis, your

earned income (at a yearly rate) was: before redistribution: $_____;

after redistribution: $_____

Task 3:   Your production: _____; group production: _____; On this basis, your

earned income (at a yearly rate) was: before redistribution: $_____;

after redistribution: $_____

Total earnings: $_____; On a yearly basis: $_____

Total payment received: $_____ (= [yearly earnings / 8320[a]] +

test money)

Signature: _____

Date: _____

[a] This constant is the amount required to convert the yearly incomes into the payment scale given in Table 5.

END-OF-PRODUCTION-PERIOD DOCUMENT

The following questions were asked of subjects after each production period:

Name _____ Before tax earnings _____
After tax income _____

1. How do you feel about your effort at the task you just completed? (Circle the appropriate answer.)
   a. much above group average
   b. a bit above group average
   c. about equal to the group average
   d. a bit below group average
   e. much below group average

2. Rank order, according to your preferences, the following 4 principles of distributive justice by placing the letters (a), (b), (c), (d), signifying the principles, in the blanks below. Indicate ties by placing the tied principles in the same space.

   most preferred _____ _____ _____ _____ least preferred
   a. maximize the floor income
   b. maximize the average income
   c. maximize the average income, subject to a floor constraint
   d. maximize the average income, subject to a range constraint

3. How do you feel about your ranking of these principles? (Circle the appropriate answer.)
   a. very unsure
   b. unsure
   c. no opinion
   d. sure
   e. very sure

4. How do you feel about your skill at the task you just completed? (Circle the appropriate answer.)
   a. much above group average
   b. a bit above group average
   c. about equal to the group average
   d. a bit below group average
   e. much below group average

5. How satisfied are you with the distributive principle selected by the group?

   a. very unsatisfied
   b. unsatisfied
   c. neither satisfied nor unsatisfied
   d. satisfied
   e. very satisfied

6. How do you feel about your performance at the task you just completed? (Circle the appropriate answer.)

   a. much above group average
   b. a bit above group average
   c. about equal to the group average
   d. a bit below group average
   e. much below group average

Setting the Imposed Principle

The principle imposed in the ten experiments in which groups were not allowed to choose was a floor constraint of $9,900. A floor constraint was selected because it was the principle most often chosen by the other groups in the basic experiment and its variants. As it turned out, in the production experiments, when discussion and choice took place, the most popular group choice was also the floor-constraint principle (see Table G1). Twelve of the eighteen groups chose that principle outright, while three groups combined it with a range constraint. Only three groups chose the principle of a range constraint. These results are roughly comparable to those obtained in the general class of experiments (Frohlich, Oppenheimer, and Eavey 1987a) except for the absence of group choices of the principle of maximum income.

The floor constraint of $9,900 was the mean of the floors chosen in the nonproduction experiments. It was not very different from the mean of the floors chosen by the subjects in the production experiments (see Table G2). Of the fifteen production groups that chose the floor-constraint principle, two did not specify a numerical value for the floor constraint but defined it as a function of properties of the income distribution.

243

Table G1. Group Choice of Principle for
         Production Experiments

Type of Experiment	Floor Constraint	Range Constraint	Total
Unanimity	11	2	13
Majority rule	4	1	5
Total	15	3	18

We examined only the thirteen numerically specified floor constraints as displayed in Table G2. Because the difference between the mean in the experiments and the imposed floor constraint is not significant, the imposed floor constraint can be treated as a reasonable approximation of that picked by subjects when they chose their own redistributional policies.

Table G2. Distribution of Floor Constraints

Number of groups	13
Mean	10,750
Standard deviation	5,426

Size of Constraint (thousands of dollars)	Each Digit Represents an Observation[a]
2	
3	6
4	
5	0
6	00
7	
8	0
9	
10	00
11	0
12	0
13	
14	0
15	07
.	
.	
.	
23	4

[a] Each digit is the number of hundreds of dollars of the choice above the thousands of dollars indicated in the left column. Thus, the 6 in the second row is a floor set at $3,600.

References

Abel, C. Frederick, and Joe A. Oppenheimer. 1982. "Liberating the Industrious Tailor." *Political Methodology*, 8, no. 1:39–60.

Aldrich, John H., and Forrest D. Nelson. 1984. *Linear Probability, Logit, and Probit Models*. Beverly Hills: Sage.

Bartlett, John. 1980. *Familiar Quotations*. 15th ed. Boston: Little, Brown.

Bierhoff, H. W., R. Cohen, and Jerald Greenberg, eds. 1986. *Justice in Social Relations*. New York: Plenum.

Bond, Douglas G., and Jong Chul Park. 1991. "An Empirical Test of Rawls' Theory of Justice: A Second Approach in Korea and the USA." *Journal of Games and Simulations* (forthcoming).

Brickman, Philip. 1977. "Preference for Inequality." *Sociometry*, 40, no. 4:303–310.

Canova, Ronnie, Ilya Gamel, Leon Gaumond, Jr., Kathy Glassman, and William Goldberg. 1990. "An Experimental Test of Role Switching as a Means of Solving the Prisoner's Dilemma." Unpublished undergraduate paper, University of Maryland, College Park.

Caws, Peter. 1967. *Science and the Theory of Value*. New York: Random House.

Chisolm, R. 1978. "Practical Reason and the Logic of Requirement." In *Practical Reasoning*, edited by Joseph Raz, 118–127. Oxford: Oxford University Press.

Darwall, Stephen L. 1983. *Impartial Reason*. Ithaca, N.Y.: Cornell University Press.

Dawes, Robyn M. 1980. "Social Dilemmas." *Annual Review of Psychology*, 31:169–193.

Dawes, Robyn M., Jeanne McTavish, and Harriet Shaklee. 1977. "Behavior, Communication and Assumptions about Other People's Behavior in a Common Dilemma Situation." *Journal of Personality and Social Psychology,* 35, no. 1:1–11.

Deutsch, Morton. 1985. *Distributive Justice: A Social-Psychological Perspective.* New Haven, Conn.: Yale.

Downs, Anthony. 1957. *An Economic Theory of Democracy.* New York: Harper & Row.

Eavey, Cheryl L., and Gary J. Miller. 1984. "Fairness in Majority Rule Games with Core." *American Journal of Political Science,* 28:570–586.

Edel, Abraham. 1963. *Method in Ethical Theory.* Indianapolis: Bobbs-Merrill.

Firth, Roderick. 1952. "Ethical Absolutism and the Ideal Observer." *Philosophy and Phenomenological Research,* 12, no. 3: 317–345.

Frohlich, Norman. 1991. "An Impartial Reasoning Solution to the Prisoners' Dilemma." *Public Choice* (forthcoming).

Frohlich, Norman, and Joe A. Oppenheimer. 1971. "I Get by with a Little Help from My Friends." *World Politics,* 22 (October): 104–121.

———. 1989. "Participation, Productivity and Stability: Experiments on Fair Democratic Income Policy Decisions." In *Operational Research and the Social Sciences,* edited by Mike Jackson, 195–200. London: Plenum.

———. 1990. "Choosing Justice in Experimental Democracies with Production." *American Political Science Review,* 84, no. 2:461–477.

Frohlich, Norman, and Joe A. Oppenheimer, with Pat Bond and Irvin Boschman. 1984. "Beyond Economic Man." *Journal of Conflict Resolution,* 28, no. 1:3–24.

Frohlich, Norman, Joe A. Oppenheimer, and Cheryl Eavey. 1987a. "Choices of Principles of Distributive Justice in Experimental Groups." *American Journal of Political Science,* 31, no. 3:606–636.

———. 1987b. "Laboratory Results on Rawls' Principle of Distributive Justice." *British Journal of Political Science,* 17:1–21.

Gewirth, Alan. 1978. "The Golden Rule Rationalized." In *Studies in Philosophy, III,* edited by Peter A. French, T. E. Vehling, Jr., and H. K. Wettstein, 133–147. Minneapolis: University of Minnesota Press.

Gleick, James. 1987. *Chaos: Making a New Science.* New York: Viking Press.

Greenberg, J., and R. L. Cohen, eds. 1982. *Equity and Justice in Social Behavior.* New York: Academic Press.

Hare, R. M. 1963. *Freedom and Reason*. Oxford: Oxford University Press.

———. 1973. "Rawls' Theory of Justice." *Philosophical Quarterly*, 21 (April and July):144–155, 241–252.

Harrison, Jonathan. 1956. "Some Comments on Professor Firth's Ideal Observer Theory." *Philosophy and Phenomenological Research*, 17:256–262.

Harsanyi, John. 1953. "Cardinal Utility in Welfare Economics and in the Theory of Risk-Taking." *Journal of Political Economy*, 61:434–435.

———. 1955. "Cardinal Welfare, Individualistic Ethics, and Interpersonal Comparisons of Utility." *Journal of Political Economy*, 63:302–321.

Hawking, Stephen W. 1988. *A Brief History of Time: From the Big Bang to Black Holes*. New York: Bantam Books.

Henberg, M. C. 1978. "Impartiality." *Canadian Journal of Philosophy*, 8, no. 4:715–724.

Hinton, William. 1966. *Fanshen: A Documentary of Revolution in a Chinese Village*. New York: Vintage.

Hochschild, Jennifer L. 1981. *What's Fair? American Beliefs about Distributive Justice*. Cambridge, Mass.: Harvard University Press.

Hoffman, Elizabeth, and Matthew Spitzer. 1985. "Entitlements, Rights, and Fairness: An Experimental Examination of Subjects' Conceptions of Distributive Justice." *Journal of Legal Studies*, 14: 259–297.

Howe, Roger E., and John E. Roemer. 1981. "Rawlsian Justice as the Core of a Game." *American Economic Review*, 71, no. 5:880–895.

Isaac, Mark, James Walker, and Arlington Williams. 1990. "Group Size and the Voluntary Provision of Public Goods." Paper presented at the annual meetings of the Public Choice Society, Tucson, Ariz.

Jasso, G. 1980. "A New Theory of Distributive Justice." *American Sociological Review*, 45 (February):3–32.

———. 1986. "A New Representation of the Just Term in Distributive Justice Theory: Its Properties and Operation in Theoretical Derivation and Empirical Estimation." *Journal of Mathematical Sociology*, 12, no. 3:251–274.

Jeffrey, Richard C. 1975. "Probability and Falsification: Critique of the Popper Program." *Synthese*, 30:95–117, and comments and replies, 118–157.

Kant, Immanuel. [1785] 1959. *The Foundations of Metaphysics of Morals*. Translated by L. W. Beck. Indianapolis: Bobbs-Merrill.

Kanter, Rosabeth M. 1987. "Pay: From Status to Contributions: Some Organizational Implications." *Personnel,* 64:12–37.

Köhler, Wolfgang. [1939] 1966. *The Place of Value in a World of Facts.* New York: Mentor.

Lakatos, I. 1970. "Falsification and the Methodology of Scientific Research Programmes." In *Criticism and the Growth of Knowledge,* edited by I. Lakatos and A. Musgrave, 91–97. Cambridge: Cambridge University Press.

Lebergott, Stanley. 1976. *The American Economy.* Princeton, N.J.: Princeton University Press.

Lewis, C. I. 1946. *An Analysis of Knowledge and Valuation.* Lasalle, Ill.: Open Court.

Lissowski, Grzegorz, Tadeus Tyszka, and Wlodzimirz Okrasa. 1991. "Principles of Distributive Justice." *Journal of Conflict Resolution,* 35, no. 1:98–119.

Marwell, Gerald, and Ruth E. Ames. 1979. "Experiments on the Provision of Public Goods (I): Resources, Interest, Group Size, and the Free Rider Problem." *American Journal of Sociology,* 84, no. 6:1335–1360.

———. 1980. "Experiments on the Provision of Public Goods (II): Provision Points, Stakes, Experience, and the Free Rider Problem." *American Journal of Sociology,* 85, no. 4:926–936.

Maxwell, Nicholas. 1972. "A Critique of Popper's Views on Scientific Method." *Philosophy of Science,* 6:131–152.

Messick, D. M., and M. B. Brewer. 1983. "Solving Social Dilemmas: A Review." *Review of Personality and Social Psychology,* 4:11–44.

Mill, John Stuart. [1844] 1967. "On the Definition of Political Economy." In *Essays on Economics and Society,* edited by J. M. Robson. Toronto: University of Toronto Press.

Miller, David. 1975. "The Accuracy of Predictions." *Synthese,* 30:159–191.

Miller, Gary J., and Joe A. Oppenheimer. 1982. "Universalism in Experimental Committees." *American Political Science Review,* 76, no. 2:561–574.

Nagel, Ernest. 1961. *The Structure of Science: Problems in the Logic of Scientific Explanation.* New York: Harcourt Brace & World.

Nagel, Thomas. 1986. *The View from No Where.* Oxford: Oxford University Press.

Nozick, Robert. 1974. *Anarchy, State and Utopia.* New York: Basic Books.

Olson, Mancur. 1965. *The Logic of Collective Action.* Cambridge, Mass.: Harvard University Press.

Plato. *The Republic.* Translated by F. M. Cornford. New York: Oxford University Press, 1945.

Popper, Karl. 1968. *The Logic of Scientific Discovery.* 2d paperback ed. New York: Harper & Row.

Rawls, John. 1971. *A Theory of Justice.* Cambridge, Mass.: Harvard University Press.

———. 1985. "Justice and Fairness: Political Not Metaphysical." *Philosophy and Public Affairs,* 14, no. 3:223–251.

Raz, Joseph, ed. 1978. *Practical Reasoning.* Oxford: Oxford University Press.

Sen, Amartya K. 1973. *On Economic Inequality.* New York: Norton.

———. 1990. "Individual Freedom as a Social Commitment." *New York Review of Books,* 37, no. 10:49–54. (Reprint of an address given at the award ceremony in Turin for the 2nd Senator Giovanni Agnelli International Prize.)

Soltan, Karol E. 1982. "Empirical Studies of Distributive Justice." *Ethics,* 92 (July):673–691.

Steinberg, Dan. 1985. *LOGIT: A Supplementary Module for Systat.* Evanston, Ill.: Salford Systems.

Toulmin, Stephen. 1972. *Human Understanding: The Collective Use and Evolution of Concepts.* Princeton, N.J.: Princeton University Press.

Transcripts (of experiments). Mimeo (349 pages). Available on paper or on flat (ASCII) text files for research and examination purposes from the authors with a charge for duplication, handling, and mailing.

Tversky, A., and D. Kahneman. 1981. "The Framing of Decisions and the Psychology of Choice." *Science* 221 (January 30):453–458.

von Neumann, John, and Oscar Morgenstern. 1948. *The Theory of Games and Economic Behavior.* Princeton, N.J.: Princeton University Press.

Von Wright, G. H. 1978. "On So Called Practical Inference." In *Practical Reasoning,* edited by Joseph Raz, 46–63. Oxford: Oxford University Press.

Williams, Bernard. 1985. *Ethics and the Limits of Philosophy.* Cambridge, Mass.: Harvard University Press.

Index